Innocent Heart, Laughter and Tears

A Memoir of Maria Marzia Maiello
And Her Family Life
In Santa Nicola La Strada, Italy

Antonia Sparano Geiser

LOST COAST PRESS
Fort Bragg
California

Innocent Heart, Laughter and Tears
A Memoir of Maria Marzia Maiello and Her
Family Life in Santa Nicola La Strada, Italy

For information, or to order additional copies, please contact:

Lost Coast Press
155 Cypress Street
Fort Bragg, California 95437
(707) 964-9520 Fax: 707-964-7531
http://www.cypresshouse.com

Cover Portrait courtesy of author's collection
Cover Design by Gopa Design

ISBN 1-882897-51-X
Library of Congress Catalog Card No.: 99-76611

Manufactured in the USA
2 4 6 8 9 7 5 3 1

First edition

Dedication

Vincenza, a grandmother whom many loved dearly

Giulio, a grandfather who loved me

Ciccillo & Mimi, two very special uncles

And to my Mother–

To return a gift bestowed upon me,

A written legacy.

Dear Reader,

In October 1997, I entered the twentieth century late, when I purchased a computer from my friend Kim. With great excitement, my husband's encouragement, and a strong desire to document an oral family history, I started to get Mom's stories down on paper. My intention was to not let them be lost to time, and to share them with the next generation of family who, not so fortunate as I, didn't hear them firsthand from my grandmother and mother. As the work progressed it became apparent that I wanted to share these stories with the families of all Americans, many of whom shared a common thread when they or their ancestors entered New York through Ellis Island as immigrants.

My mother, Maria Marzia, the main character in this book, has been an inspiration. With due respect, this is her memoir and I took the liberty of putting her part of the story in the first person. Without her there would be no book.

When I first embarked on this journey, I didn't realize how vast Mom's memory was or how much I wanted to please her by doing this work with her. I failed to realize that we would be opening Pandora's Box. We have cried and laughed into the late hours of many nights. Although Pandora's initial action left her no choice in releasing all the ills into the world, I exercised free will and chose to omit some stories, simply out of respect for Mom and our extensive family. New knowledge brought empowerment, old faded family pictures and stories came alive with explanation, understanding, tears and sometimes acceptance. Childhood questions were finally answered, and situations brought to closure.

Grandfather Giulio died when I was two years old, and the few memories that I have of my very early years do not include him. But I do know from many relatives that I was very special to him. If my birth was the instrument to change hearts, and my young life the bridge from pain to love and forgiveness, then that is reason in itself for my involvement in this story.

I'm mourning once again for Grandma Vincenza, remembering mostly my love for her and her laughter. She was so special. I was blessed to have her in my life until I was thirty years old, and felt with her passing the loss of connection to my Italian heritage and a door closing on a chapter of personal history.

As children, my sisters and I asked for stories about Italy. We were intrigued with the relatives we never met, the places we hadn't seen and the language we weren't taught because our Neapolitan parents wanted us to be Americans.

My father, Tony, was born in America but spent much of his youth in Italy. His father, an importer of wine and other items, traveled every few years with his whole family between Italy and America. Dad grew up in the Town of San Benedetto, which is so close to Caserta and my mother's birthplace, Santa Nicola, that as a youth he played soccer with her friend's older brothers! But my parents didn't meet in Italy; they met here in Brooklyn and that is another story.

So these are the stories I heard from my earliest childhood as Mom and Grandma told them to me. Some made me cry; others charmed me. Some still have the ability to scare me, and a few humbled me with a great respect for my ancestors, who faced adversity and survived despite the circumstances. They arrived from Italy with dignity and their indomitable spirits. With a strong work ethic, intelligence and perseverance they became proud American citizens. They brought their stories, and shared them to keep the memory of Italy alive in their hearts, repeating them lovingly and always with laughter and tears.

ASG
August 1999

Table of Contents

GLOSSARY

Acqua de Serena Water, clear and beneficial

Befana Old fairy or ugly old woman from Italian, Epifania

Bella Feminine: Beauty

Benevento Town in Naples area; Strega, an Italian liquor, is made there

Braciole Plural: thinly sliced beef, rolled and stuffed with chopped garlic, fresh parsley, tied and sautéed for the sauce

Brutto Masculine; ugly

Buon Natale Merry Christmas

Buona Pasqua Easter Holiday

Caffeteria Cafeteria, coffee shop

Caiazzo Mountain town in Naples area

Carrozzino A light carriage

Cartolina Postcard

Cipolla An onion

Denari Money, Roman denarius

Destino Mio My fate, or my destiny

E' la commedia e' finita The play, or comedy, is over

Epifania The Epiphany, January 6th

Fantasima A ghost or phantom

Funiculi, Funicula Transport up and down a mountain; ski lift

Fernet Branca "bitters" or beneficial herbs mixed with alcohol, used medicinally

Gelati Lemon ices, ice cream

Ivangilista Evangelist, as in St. Mark

Lavoritrice Worker; female worker, singular; woman

Mal Occhio The Evil Eye

Mammono Bogeyman

Masculoni Masculine

Mazzamauriello Little impish men

Mulino Mill

Napoli Naples, Italy

Nonna Grandmother

Nonno Grandfather

Ossuario Ossuary, receptacle for bones of the dead, charnel house, tomb

Padrone Master or Boss

Palazzo Palace

Paoliso A town in Benevento Province, where witches were reputed to be

Prosciutto A cured ham, spicy and peppery

Puttanesca A tomato sauce, a whore's recipe

Pozzuoli A town near Naples

Pupetta Little girl or doll

Sanguinaccio A pork blood pudding

Scifato Neapolitan: to find repulsive, sickening, turning one's stomach

Strega A witch. Also, an Italian liquor, "witches brew" made in the Town of Benevento

Vecchia old, Feminine

Vecchio old, Masculine

Zampogna Reed pipe, bagpipe

Zia Aunt

Zingara A gypsy, feminine singular

Zingari Gypsies, plural

Zio Uncle

IN THE CAMPANIA REGION

Thirty-two kilometers north of Naples

In the vicinity of Mt. Vesuvius, inland from the Mediterranean Sea, lies the Town of Santa Nicola La Strada, on the outskirts of the city of Caserta.

Naples, or Napoli, as it is called now, was named by Greek settlers who populated the area hundreds of years before the birth of Christ. They called it "Neapolis," or New City. Taken from the Greeks by the Romans, the port of Naples was used from ancient times. Romans prized the area for its great beauty and clement weather.

Throughout the ages, the area was also prized by the European nobility and by a branch of the Bourbons, an extensive royal family with roots in France. The earliest documented member of the French branch was a feudal lord in the late 9th century. Through generations, marital alliances, wars and political takeovers, the Spanish branch and, later, the Neapolitan branch were formed.

The son of King Philip V of Spain was Carlos de Borbon (later Charles III of Spain), who founded the Neapolitan house of Bourbon by becoming the King of the Two Sicilies. He conquered and ruled as Charles IV between 1734 and 1759. In 1759, Charles acceded to the Spanish throne and made his younger son King Ferdinand IV of Naples.

In 1752, Charles IV commissioned the Italian architect Luigi Vanvitelli to build a royal palace (Palazzo Reale) for him in Caserta, twenty miles north of Naples. Vanvitelli built this palace from 1752 until his death at age seventy-three. His son completed the palace in 1774.

The Palazzo Reale was immense; larger than the Palace at Versailles, France, with four interior courtyards and nearly twelve hundred rooms. Vanvitelli, master of interior effects, created long vistas, endless sequences of rooms, and glimpses of courtyards and waterfalls from long staircases, all in late Baroque style.

Because of Santa Nicola's close proximity to the City of Caserta, situated across the railroad tracks and within walking distance, the townspeople took great pride in Caserta's great palace. Palazzo Reale, with its beauty and history of Bourbon Kings, was a thing of pride for everyone in the surrounding area. As with anything great, stories and legends surround it. According to the legend told for generations by the Neapolitans, Luigi Vanvitelli, its builder, promised it would rival the Palace of Versailles. Upon its completion, he was asked if he could ever create such beauty again.

He responded, "Yes."

Asked to compare it to Versailles, he said, "It is even more beautiful than the Palace of Versailles," whereupon they put out his eyes so that he could never again create such magnificent beauty as he had with Palazzo Reale.

FROM KINGDOM TO DICTATORSHIP

Humberto I was King of Italy from 1878 to 1900. Before his reign, he had fought bravely for the unification of Italy, serving as an army captain in several battles against the Austrians.

In 1882, during Humberto's reign as King, he was involved in the signing of a military defense pact known as the Triple Alliance, with Germany and Austria-Hungary. This alliance was the official beginning of the division of Europe, which eventually resulted in the outbreak of World War I in 1914.

In 1900, Neapolitan-born Victor Emmanuel III became King of Italy after his father's assassination by an anarchist. In 1915 he brought Italy into World War I on the side of the allied powers, and spent three years on active duty at the Asiago front in northern Italy. When the war ended in 1918, the reconstruction in Italy was marked by political and industrial strife.

Largely self-educated, Benito Mussolini was a schoolteacher who became a journalist and editor of Avanti, the Socialist Party newspaper in Milan. He was jailed for his opposition to Italy's war in Libya during 1911 and 1912. When WW I began, he was opposed to the "imperialist war," but soon changed his mind and called for an allied entry for Italy. For this he was expelled from the Socialist Party, whereupon he started his own newspaper in Milan, calling it Il Popolo d'Italia. This paper later became the voice of the Fascist Party.

In 1919, Mussolini, an ex-soldier and former socialist, founded the Fasci di Combattimento, a nationalistic, anti-liberal and anti-socialistic group. He coined the term Fascism from the ancient Roman fasces, a symbol of discipline denoted by a bundle of sticks bound to an ax. This symbol represented civic unity and the power of Roman officials to punish wrongdoers. He organized the Black Shirt paramilitary squads into the official militia of the Fascist Party.

Extremely nationalistic, fascism employed violence to suppress any opposition. Within a year it spread through the countryside, with Black Shirt militia winning support from landowners and attacking peasant leagues and socialist groups.

In 1922, following the collapse of parliamentary government, King Victor Emmanuel III, refusing to declare martial law, accepted the Fascist regime of Benito Mussolini. A coalition government was formed to avoid civil war when the Fascists threatened to march on Rome.

By 1925 Mussolini, now Il Duce, had seized total control of the Italian government, establishing himself as dictator. Il Duce banned all political parties except his Fascist Party. Labor unions were abolished, strikes forbidden, and political opponents immediately silenced.

This story takes place during the King's time, and during the changes brought about by the encroachment of fascism and the growing power of Mussolini.

Let us journey together a little while,

We will travel back to another time,

Perhaps a simpler place.

To an old-world homeland whispering,

Far across the north Atlantic Ocean

And the warm Mediterranean Sea.

Take a sunlit horse and buggy ride
overland from the Bay of Naples,

Always keep your eye on Mt. Vesuvius in the distance,

And look for fields and fields of poppies
blooming in the spring.

When we arrive at the railroad junction in Caserta,

And cross over the tracks to the Via Santa Croce

We will know in our hearts

That together in Santa Nicola,

We have finally returned home.

Circle closed back to the beginning.

PROLOGUE: 1920
A BITTER LESSON TO LEARN

Giulio Maiello's passport picture, 1920

The Beginning of a Bitter Lesson

Santa Nicola La Strada—March 23, 1920

When Papa Giulio left for America the second time, he was almost twenty-five years old. He left Mamma Vincenza, then twenty-three, to raise the three of us alone. I was only fifteen days old.

Mamma always said that her early years in Italy with Papa were good ones. Papa's intention was to work for one year in America and then return home rich. The general belief at the time was that money could be plucked from trees in America. When Papa left, Mamma had tremendous support, coupled with great love, from her in-laws, the Maiello family. Mamma and Papa's years together were only to be interrupted by this one, while he worked in America, or so they thought.

Mamma's father, Papa Sebastiano Veccia, stepped in when Papa Giulio left. He asked Mamma to return to work and run the grocery store for him. So once again Mamma had a steady income. She and Papa corresponded often, but she never received very much money from him. She sustained us with her income from the grocery store.

While Mamma worked, I spent my early days with my brothers, Francesco (Ciccillo) and Domenico (Mimi), at the Veccia's house under their supervision. We had our meals with Papa Sebastiano and Mamma Raffaela. We spent our nights with Mamma in the Maiello palazzo, to be near Nonna Marzia. Papa Giulio had inherited our bedroom from his father, Francesco.

When Papa Giulio arrived in America, he knew that he had to find work right away or starve. He left the docks of New York and went to

Pennsylvania to work in the coal mines. He wrote Mamma that the mines were very dangerous, wet and dirty.

That job lasted only one day; it just wasn't for him! When Papa left Pennsylvania, he went to Brooklyn, New York, and found work in the building trades. He learned scaffold building. Because of his talent and his perfectionism he was soon put in charge of others. He started to do quite well for himself. As a foreman he gave jobs to all his fellow townsmen who arrived in Brooklyn from Santa Nicola. He generously sent baskets of food anonymously to families when he heard their children were hungry. He established himself and made a life in America without us.

Mamma and both sides of the family raised us quite well in Santa Nicola. Grandparents, uncles, aunts and cousins surrounded us. Mamma had her family, her brother Rocco, her work in the store, and wonderful friendships with her sisters-in-law and neighbors. The town was a good place to raise children. My brothers and I spent many happy days in Italy. We grew with love and laughter in the Neapolitan sunshine. Like the poppies in the fields around us, we matured with strong roots, blossomed and endured, but without our Papa. What was thought to be only a temporary separation became almost eleven years with Papa in America, the years passing without him in our lives.

I grew to learn a very hard lesson in Italy: I learned that a little girl needed her Papa. I didn't even know mine. My desire for him was flamed by his absence. It was my secret sorrow that I yearned for his return home. My sorrow grew as each year passed, from hope to empty, bitter loss.

Those early years were the years I needed him the most.

INNOCENT HEART, LAUGHTER AND TEARS

A Memoir of Maria Marzia Maiello
And Her Family Life
In Santa Nicola La Strada, Italy

SANTA NICOLA LA STRADA

Vincenza Veccia at age fourteen

1910

Santa Nicola was a suburban town with five streets. The only greenery in town was along the Via Santa Croce. Behind the town, from the rear windows of the stone houses, you could see farms in the distance. There were many stores, including a cigar store, a dressmaker, a men's shop, two shoemakers, a barber shop, a grocery store, a bakery, two butcher shops, and a fabric store that sold yard goods on the Via San Marco. There were also two fresh produce stores with fruit and vegetables displayed out front, and a farm you could walk to using the driveway behind the church, past the mausoleum wall of buried priests.

Everyone in town knew everyone else. Strangers were seldom seen, and most doors were kept unlocked during the days, bolted only at night. The townspeople were for the most part good, decent, and hardworking, neighborly yet respectful of others' privacy. Not gossipy or backward, they all knew what they were about. If by some twist of fate a simpleton was born in town, he was left alone and not taunted.

The church was always the center of life in town, and down the Via Santa Croce, before it turned by the public water fountain to the Palazzo Santoro, was "the Circle of Santa Nicola." The circle was a meeting place for men and the town elders to discuss church matters. The church was always involved with the people in town, too. When the discussions were finally done the men played a friendly card game or smoked a cigar. It was their ritual.

The environment was perfect for crops, with a long, hot summer growing season, short winter months, and very rich and fertile soil. The community had horses, mules, donkeys, chickens, pigs, and even stray dogs and cats that would hang around the wells.

The only animals that came close to being pets were pigeons. They sometimes came into the houses and some people kept them as pets. On occasion they were also used to make a special soup for "new mothers only" in the belief that it was specially nourishing.

Santa Nicola was an old town steeped in lore and legends. If you heard of someone found dead, slashed to death, it was probably werewolves that killed him.

Witch stories were told: if morning arrived and you found your horse's hair all braided, tail and mane, witches had been there to bother you the night before. And if someone found a doll in the well, made with a lemon head and with pins stuck all over the cloth body, then the person the doll resembled would die when the lemon rotted. The woman who had made the doll would be sure that her intended victim would hear the news and die of fright!

The storytellers always talked of "little men" who left money in the houses that they visited. These little men were called *Mazzamauriello*, and if you left bread and water out for them, they would treat you to a reward of gold!

"Little Men" and Lost Treasure

When Mamma Vincenza was young girl, she moved with her family from her birthplace, the City of Caserta, to Santa Nicola. They went to live in a house on the Via Santa Croce. Papa Sebastiano's bakery and bread store was on the first floor, where the kitchen was. Mamma Raffaela cooked the family's meals and served them on the large bread table in the bakery. Across the courtyard was a small garden, and stairs to the second floor, where there was an open verandah with two large bedrooms, a bathroom and a sitting room. The sitting room and the bathroom were on either end of the verandah, their doors facing each other, the two bedrooms between them. The sitting room had a window where pigeons roosted at night, and in the ceiling a trap door leading to an attic that no one ever went into. Vincenza was afraid of the attic, and in her fear she imagined all kinds of horrible things about it. The children's bedroom had a balcony facing the street and was closest to the bathroom.

One day, Raffaela planned to take Vincenza to visit her sister Maria Antonia in the Town of Caiazzo the next day. At night the family turned off all the oil lamps and retired to their beds. In the middle of the night Vincenza awakened to the loud screeching of pigeons. Something had awakened them. An oil lamp was alight, even though all the lamps had been extinguished when they had retired. Then she saw a little man, *Mazzamauriello*, looking at her, walking back and forth and pointing at something in the bedroom end table. Terrified, she kept her eyes shut tightly.

When finally she realized that he had gone, she called to her father to come right away and bring her clothes. She told her parents about seeing *Mazzamauriello*, and insisted they should take her to Zia Maria Antonia's house right away. She was very upset and frightened. She said that she would never come back to the family until they moved out of that house!

Her father didn't believe her. Her siblings; Rocco, Filomena, Carolina and Nicola, sleeping in the same room, didn't see or hear anything. But early the next morning he dressed and took Vincenza to her aunt's house.

When they arrived at Zia Maria Antonia's and told her what had happened, she insisted that they all return home so that Vincenza could check the night table for any gold reward that was left for her. She said that the reward was meant only for Vincenza and she had to be the person to look for it. Vincenza would have nothing to do with it. She stayed with her aunt and her parents returned home without her.

A few weeks later, with Vincenza safely at her aunt's house, the family turned off all the oil lamps and retired to their beds. In the middle of the night, Sebastiano heard the pigeons making a racket in the sitting room. Again something had disturbed them. He went to investigate and found the oil lamp lit and a little man dancing around the table!

He said to the little man, "In the name of God, who are you?"

The little man danced around the table and didn't answer.

He repeated, "In the name of God, who are you?"

Again he received no answer, and the little man continued to dance around the table.

Finally, in a very loud voice, Sebastiano commanded a third time, "In God's name, who are you?"

At that point *Mazzamauriello* stopped dancing, blew into Sebastiano's face and disappeared!

Mazzamauriello was never seen again. Vincenza spent a month at her aunt's house, not returning to her family until they rented rooms at the Maiello Palazzo. And in spite of her aunt's repeated pleas, Vincenza never looked in the end table by the side of her bed in her old room.

Vincenza eventually went to work in her father's new grocery store in Santa Nicola. She worked hard to please her family, and her father soon gave her great responsibilities. She was so business-minded and competent she was running the store by the age of fourteen.

Sixteen-year-old Giulio Maiello began to notice her. Vincenza didn't like the attention, and commented to people that when she had to pass him to get to work, her legs shook so much she wasn't sure if she could make it. She was so shy, she blushed just talking about it.

But the attention continued until Giulio was absolutely crazy about Vincenza. When his papa, Francesco, noticed Giulio's attraction to Vincenza, he commented, "You sure know how to pick them!" He was very pleased with his son's choice.

THE MAIELLO'S

Coat of Arms

Original Name: Maioli
Origin: Faenza and Ravenna, Italy
Date of Origin: Possibly 1160
Classification: Nobles
Derivatives and variations: Maiorello, Maiella, Maiello, Maella
Arms: Per Fess Or and Asure.
In chief: a two-headed eagle, sable. Each head crowned of the field.
In base: three fleur-de-lis, argent or;* in good order.

History

Maioli family information prior to the move from Faenza to Ravenna in the early 1500s is limited at best. The shape and design of the coat of arms is that of the earliest bearer of heraldic cognizance, dating back to the year 1150. My own research at the main office of the New York Public Library leads me to believe that the arms was granted around 1160 to an advocate named Placido. The accompanying information, taken from the encyclopedia and the *History of Italian Nobility*, by G.B. Crollalanza, traces the history of certain prominent Maioli family members who remained in or around Ravenna, dating from the 1500s to the mid 1600s. Granted to the Maioli Family in Ravenne, Italy. The Noble Family changed residence from Paenza to Ravenna around the turn of the 15th century. Soon after, the family began to distinguish itself.

Giovanni, born in the year 1591, was a poet of distinguished fame. Serafina, a nun of St. Andrea, 1570, was also a poetess of merit. Agostino, a generous man of noble heart, died in the year 1693, having lived almost one hundred years. Giuseppe, Agostino's brother, was treasurer of Romagna. Giacomo Maioli was elected chief magistrate, which was the city's highest position, for three terms: 1617, 1621 and 1643. Little information appears to be available relative to those who migrated or whose surnames evolved.

* The Certificate of Authenticity provided by the Sanson Institute describes the three fleur-de-lis as "argent" (silver). The description accompanying the arms illustration on page 233 of the encyclopedia, however, describes them as "or" (gold).

G. Maiello

Paternal Grandparents

Francesco Maiello and Marzia Sparaco Maiello

Francesco and Marzia lived in a seventeen-room palazzo with their ten children. Francesco was a winemaker and traveled from town to town selling barrels of wine.

In front of the palazzo, to the left of the front door, was an attached building dedicated to making wine. Access to this area was either through the alleyway entrance that had wrought iron gates, or from the courtyard, through the big storage rooms. A statue of Bacchus was on the roof overlooking the courtyard.

The family's farms produced grapes for wine, and vegetables, wheat, and flax for weaving. Francesco's winepress was so large it filled that first floor room in the palazzo. Both the adjacent rooms and the wine cellar were used for wine storage. Next to the wine cellar entrance were the work kitchen and the horse barns.

Francesco's workers turned the winepress, crushed the grapes and then stored the new barrels of wine in the wine cellar. The cellar staircase was bordered with flat horizontal sides wide enough to accommodate the width of the wine barrels. The workers lowered the barrels down the staircase with ropes.

Whenever Francesco returned from a business trip he asked his wife Marzia why she looked angry. She would pout and he would ask, "Why are you unhappy?" Then, he called her Padrone, and before she could answer him, he told her to hold her apron up. He threw coins into it and said, "Here, are you happy now?" He filled her apron with money! He treated her very well and even spoiled her; he loved her so much.

Marzia missed her husband when he went on his trips. The responsibility of the business operations and her children kept her very busy. She prepared food for all the farm workers and spent her days cooking and baking large rounds of bread to feed them three meals a day.

Marzia was small and delicate but strong-willed. She was hardworking, energetic and very talented. And, when Marzia didn't get her own way, she pretended to faint!

Giulio Maiello, age sixteen

Giulio and the Ghost

When Giulio was sixteen years old he slept in a room with all his brothers. During that time a farm worker with a most magnificent singing voice passed through town at 4:00 a.m. on his way to work in the fields. He sang all the way to work and all the townspeople waited to hear him.

One night, Giulio lay awake in bed waiting to hear the singing farm worker, when through the doorway to the bedroom came a woman in an old-fashioned dress and headpiece.

She walked between the beds where his brothers lay sleeping and said to Giulio, "I know that you are awake, give my salutations to your Papa."

She then disappeared! Giulio, realizing that it was a ghost, was terrified!

Later that morning, when Giulio told his papa, Francesco, about his experience and described the woman he saw, his father said, "That was my mother!"

Papa Francesco died two weeks later from double pneumonia. Giulio never got over his father's death.

Marzia's Strength

When Francesco died at the age of forty-one, he left his thirty-eight-year-old wife Marzia pregnant with their eleventh child. Everyone was devastated. Marzia picked herself up, shook out the apron her husband used to fill with money when he returned home from his business trips, and started to make plans.

She brought her baby to term and named him Francesco, after her dead husband. She then tried to collect the money owed on her husband's business accounts, but was unsuccessful because much of his business was done only by word of mouth and a handshake. The wine business fell apart. Her sons who were still living at home were too young to handle it, and all of the younger children had been living off the fat of the land. None of them worked. Only her son Filippo worked the farms, as overseer.

Marzia then concentrated on the farms with the vegetables, wheat and flax. She bought a baling machine to expand the farm business.

She was able to keep the farm workers on their jobs and continue the family business.

To avoid becoming a burden to their mother, some of the older children decided to find their own way in life. Marzia's daughter Addolorada had already married. Domenico and Angela Maria went to Brazil, and Giulio left for North America.

Marzia's Older Children

Filippo worked the fields as overseer, but was banished from the Maiello palazzo because of his relationship with a married woman.

Addolorada had a husband who came from the town of San Marco Ivangilista, a neighboring town of Santa Nicola. She had married into a farming family and she and her husband had two sons. They had a beautiful handmade bedroom set with carved angels on the chifforobe.

Her husband eventually left for America alone, leaving Addolorada to raise her two sons and work the farms with his family. She saw her brother, Filippo, in the fields at times, but never when she returned home to visit. Sometimes, when she came home to Santa Nicola, her sisters found her sitting on the church steps all alone. They told her to go back home, but her husband was gone and she missed him very much. It was no fun for Addolorada, living under her mother-in-law's thumb and raising her sons alone. Her family could see that she was unhappy; they commented that all work and no play was miserable.

Many years later her husband returned from America.

Domenico was the musical one in the family. He could pick up any instrument and play it. He sang along as he played the mandolin or guitar.

After their father died, there was no more music, just survival. Domenico went to Brazil in 1912. He had rich cousins there who promised to set him up with a meat market, and true to their word, did so when he arrived. Domenico did quite well with his business in Brazil, and once he was established he wrote to his mother Marzia that she should make arrangements to send his seventeen-year-old girlfriend Maria from Santa Nicola. He would send passage money, and because of her youth, she would need a chaperone for the journey.

His Mamma Marzia wrote back, "NO!" Maria was below Domenico's station in life and not good enough for him!

After Domenico received that letter, he never contacted his mother again. He only wrote to his sisters and brothers.

Eventually, Domenico met and fell deeply in love with a beautiful Portuguese woman named Serafina. Serafina and her sisters were considered Brazil's three most beautiful women. Domenico and Serafina married and Domenico sent pictures of their wedding to his hometown. Eventually he also sent pictures of his children to his siblings, but he never wrote to his mother Marzia again.

Despite Domenico's avoidance of his mother, he was greatly noted for his generosity. He once took a starving artist home with him. When the artist got back on his feet, he repaid Domenico for his kindness by painting oil portraits of his whole family for him.

After their father died, Giulio's older sister Angela Maria went to Brazil for one year. She happily returned to her hometown, missing it and her family. She learned many things during her visit to Brazil, and took her younger siblings under control and put them to work. She had her younger brother Pietro (Petrucci) study to become a mechanic, and guided little Francesco to apply himself toward a career. She was instrumental in getting the family back in shape after their father Francesco's death, and was a great help to her mother.

Angela Maria was a beautiful woman. She was quite fastidious about herself and wouldn't leave the house without wearing her hat and gloves. She was quite a lady.

When she met the man who became her husband, Michele Ianniello, he was just as fastidious about himself. They made the perfect couple. He owned a haberdashery in the city of Caserta and dressed quite well for his business. He made a great impression on her, and she married him when she was in her late thirties. They settled in the city to be near his business, and had only one daughter, whom they called Pupetta.

At the same time, Giulio left for North America at the age of sixteen. Vincenza's brother Rocco went too. Rocco stayed with relatives when he arrived, but soon learned that he didn't like America. He returned to Italy at about the same time that Giulio did, one year after they had left.

When Giulio returned home, his mamma sent him to work with his brother, Filippo, overseeing the farm workers. Giulio was too easy on them. Filippo complained to their mother that Giulio let the farm hands stretch out their noon meal hour.

In his own defense, Giulio said, "The sun was too hot and it burned the top of their heads, and after all they were only resting."

He was quickly taken off the overseer job.

GIULIO MAIELLO AND VINCENZA VECCIA

A Marriage

Giulio had his eye on Vincenza for years, and returned to find her still living with her family in the palazzo and working in the grocery store. He was crazy about her, but commented to her brother Rocco that "The girls in America were beautiful!"

When he heard this, Rocco was very upset. He went quickly to his Papa Sebastiano and said, "Never let this marriage take place! Why would he comment to me about the girls in America if he has an eye on my sister?"

But eventually the marriage did take place. Giulio was twenty years old and Vincenza was eighteen. The newlyweds took their entitled room at the Maiello palazzo, and Vincenza left her work at the grocery store to stay home and become a wife.

Giulio tried to find his niche in life as a married man, but he was very young. One of his first jobs was night watchman in a cemetery. The cemetery had a caretaker's cottage with a bedroom for his use once he finished his work in the late evening.

One night he fell asleep and was dreaming. Suddenly there was a loud knock at the door. He watched the door open by itself, and through the opening he saw two hands holding a heart. He heard a voice say, "Take my heart and let me in!" Terrified, he ran all the way home. That was the end of that job!

Many neighbors in Santa Nicola worked out of town. Unless you were a peasant farm worker, or owned a shop and worked as a shop-keeper, or worked for the railroad that ran between Caserta and Santa Nicola, there weren't many jobs available in the area. It wasn't unusual for men to go away to work, traveling even as far as Libya, North Africa. And there was always America, with the hope and promise of "plucking money from trees." The townspeople became more knowledgeable about the world around them as they listened to the stories of the returned workers.

When one of Giulio and Vincenza's neighbors returned home from a far-off job, the first thing he asked his wife was whether she knew of any problems with their friend, the cop?

When his wife asked him why, the husband replied, "I just saw him sitting on the ground by a water fountain. He looked up at me and seemed to be angry about something."

His wife said, "He was killed near that fountain weeks ago!"

So Giulio continued to look for work, and Vincenza kept herself busy in the palazzo. She sewed on the machines in the family kitchen and also helped bake bread for the farm workers. Since there were so many townspeople with relatives working out of town, she helped them with their letters. She was the go-between for letters that arrived from America. She read them and helped write the replies. She also started corresponding with Giulio's brother Domenico and his wife Serafina in Brazil. She did much of this work at night by oil lamplight. She was so busy that the days weren't long enough for her.

Giulio and Vincenza's first son was born on June 21, 1916, and was named after Giulio's father, Francesco. Vincenza always called him Ciccillo.

Across from the Palazzo was a Cantina

In years past, the cantina was an active bar and grill, run by the owner-proprietor until one night when he prepared himself for some unsavory clientele. He was scared of a certain group of men and thought they might show up that night. He put a knife in his apron pocket, but, so as not to rip his apron, he put the handle down first in the deep pocket. When he went downstairs to the cellar for wine, he tripped and fell. The knife stabbed him and he died instantly. His wife was so upset about her husband's death that she just abandoned the business, leaving her husband's blood on the cellar stairs.

After a while, she decided to rent the cantina. She offered it to Giulio and Vincenza. Since Giulio was still trying to find his niche in life, they decided to try opening the cantina. Every time Vincenza returned from the cellar, she watched a frog jump up the stairs ahead of her. The frog disappeared at the top step!

One time, Giulio went down to the cellar to get some wine. On his return, he was pinned behind the door at the top of the steps. He was trapped between the door and sash. He felt that something pressed the door on him and he screamed for help!

"Get this door away from me!" he yelled.

Vincenza and Ciccillo ran to help. She saw his predicament but couldn't figure out a way to help him. Ciccillo, who was about two years old at the time, asked his Papa if it was a mammono holding him. He said, "I'll make him go away!" He tapped the door three times and said, "Go away, mammono!" At that point the door opened by itself. Giulio got right out fast!

After that incident, one of the townspeople dreamed that the dead proprietor came to him and said, "My blood is still on the stairs!" When the wife of the dead proprietor heard of the townsman's dream, she took it as an omen. Too afraid to do anything about it herself, she approached Giulio and Vincenza and said, "You can have the store for nothing if you sweep up the blood and soil on the cellar stairs, bring it to the cemetery, and light a candle on the cellar steps every night."

They wanted no part of it. They abandoned the cantina, never to return.

Curtained-Off Bedroom

Each Maiello family member was entitled to a room at the palazzo. The rest of the rooms in the house were rented out to tenants. Giulio and Vincenza had a very large bedroom at the top of the stairs. Vincenza curtained off part of it to make a sitting room.

Their second son was born on January 7, 1918 and named Domenico. Vincenza always called this son Mimi.

One night, while her husband and sons slept in the bedroom area, Vincenza received some of her friends in the sitting room area. The young women sat together, sewing and enjoying their visit. They all whispered so as not to wake Giulio and the sleeping children.

When Giulio awakened, he heard the women whispering. Being nosy, he went to peek over the curtain; he thought they were whispering about him! One of Vincenza's guests, surprised to see his face looking over the curtain, got scared and screamed.

Giulio quickly jumped back into bed and covered his head with the sheet. The children had awakened with the scream and started crying. The women went with Vincenza to investigate and to console the children while Giulio, to hide himself, pulled the sheet further over his head.

Then the women all started to scream louder and louder until, finally, Giulio looked down to discover that the sheet that he thought covered his head was actually the muslin nightshirt he was wearing. Unknowingly, he had exposed himself!

After that night, Giulio walked through town with his head down. Vincenza had a big laugh about it.

The Typhus Epidemic

Sebastiano and Raffaela had left their rental room at the Maiello palazzo when Giulio and Vincenza married. They rented three rooms in the house with the grocery store in front. This house was on the Via Santa Croce, around the bend in the road from the house with the bakery and bread store, where Vincenza, as a young girl, had seen the little man, *Mazzamauriello.*

In Europe during World War I, 150 thousand soldiers had died of epidemic typhus. This infectious disease was ravaging in both Europe and America. In 1918, Giulio was working out of town. Vincenza became ill with typhus. Her two sisters were also sick. Raffaela ran back and forth between the two houses, trying to care for her three sick daughters and give them meals.

Little Ciccillo was brought back to the Veccia house so Raffaela could watch him while she nursed her two daughters at home. The infant Mimi, who was still breast-feeding, stayed with Vincenza. She was so ill she passed blood with her breast milk, but neither child became infected with typhus.

Aside from Raffaela, only Giulio's brother Filippo's woman visited Vincenza and brought her cool, fresh water. Everyone else stayed away, afraid of contracting the disease.

Vincenza and her two sisters finally recovered. Their high fevers broke after many weeks of suffering.

Labor Pains and Midwives

Vincenza said that labor pains were sweet! She never understood other women's stories of pain and screaming. She thought them foolish to complain.

In those years, babies were born in the house, with a midwife in attendance. Out of respect, the children were named for a relative, either living or dead. When Giulio and Vincenza's second son was born he was named after Giulio's older brother, who lived in Brazil.

Vincenza gave birth to Ciccillo (Francesco) and Mimi (Domenico), attended both times by a midwife. When her third child was due to arrive, they sent to Caserta for the midwife. By the time the midwife walked from Caserta to the palazzo in Santa Nicola, Vincenza had already given birth to her daughter.

She told the midwife, "I did it all by myself!"

Vincenza chose the name of her mother-in-law, Marzia, and Giulio added Maria to it because he hated the name Marzia.

So I came to be called Maria Marzia.

Vincenza Veccia Maiello

1920:
MARIA MARZIA MAIELLO

Maternal Grandparents

Sebastiano Veccia and Raffaela Petrucci Veccia

My earliest memories were of two mammas, one during the day and one at night. Mamma Vincenza brought us from the Maiello palazzo every morning to her parents' apartment above the grocery store before she went downstairs to work. Mamma Raffaela took care of us and I loved her. She was a peaceful, quiet and loving woman. My brothers and I called her *Mamma Vecchia* (Old Mamma) out of respect, and to differentiate between her and our young Mamma, Vincenza (*Mamma Giona.*) Mamma Raffaela was so respected in town that she became *Mamma Vecchia* to everyone, a title of respect.

Mamma Raffaela had the most beautiful skin. She had her hairdresser come every morning to touch up her gray roots and pile her hair into a bun high on her head. She was very soft and sweet. I was her pet and felt treasured and loved by her.

We called Papa Sebastiano *Papa Vecchio* (Old Papa), and referred to our Papa Giulio in America as *Papa Giono* (Young Papa). Papa Sebastiano was our father figure while Papa Giulio was away living in America.

When Papa Sebastiano traveled to the Town of Santa Maria to work in his bread store or to shop for supplies he needed for his stores in Santa Nicola, he returned home quite late and very tired. We greeted him with love, and helped him remove his shoes. My brothers and I held him in great regard, and we deeply respected and loved him.

Papa Sebastiano was a very holy man. He was greatly respected by the townspeople. They came to him for advice. He was saintly and learned and much involved in the church. When he was asked about the existence of God, Papa Sebastiano replied, "If there is nothing when we die, what is the harm? We have been better people to family and friends, we have lost nothing." His religion was strong and he lived by it, doing good to his fellow man.

Mamma Raffaela and Papa Sebastiano were a perfect couple with great love and devotion between them. They were kind and loving to each other and everyone else.

Papa Sebastiano's mother had died very young. His father couldn't work and raise five children also, so he put them into an orphanage. When Papa Sebastiano was young, he was playing marbles with other boys in a courtyard. One of the boys got angry with him for winning and threw a pen at him. It blinded him in one eye.

Mamma Raffaela was deaf in one ear because of a childhood illness. Unmarried at twenty-six, she was considered a spinster. Her parents felt that she wouldn't find a husband, but they didn't want her to be alone.

Papa Sebastiano's father wanted his one-eyed son to make a good marriage. The two families agreed that their children should meet. It was a perfect match! They fell in love, and married in 1893. No one ever heard a harsh word from either of them, and their love for each other deepened and grew with their years together. Theirs was truly a blessed union.

Papa Sebastiano and Mamma Raffaela's early marriage years together brought children. My Zio Rocco was born first, then, on January 20, 1897, Mamma Vincenza.

When Mamma Vincenza was five years old she had to have an operation to remove a large tumor under her arm. The surgery was performed in their home. The doctor had to go in through her side by removing one rib.

While the operation took place, her parents prayed to every saint in heaven that she might live, because they loved her very much. Mamma survived the operation, but it was a miracle that she lived. She was left with a scar and a hole in her chest from the missing rib.

Throughout the rest of her life she was held in high regard by her family because they loved her and had almost lost her.

Papa Sebastiano lost his temper only once in his lifetime. Papa Sebastiano and Mamma Raffaela had three more children after Mamma Vincenza: two daughters, named Carolina and Filomena, and their youngest child, a son they called Nicola.

Before Nicola was born, the four children, led by Rocco, were playing and running around the dining table. One of them knocked over an oil lamp, breaking its glass chimney. Papa Sebastiano replaced it. That same night it happened again. Papa Sebastiano had another broken glass chimney. He got angry and started chasing the children around the table. Mamma Vincenza, who was about six years old at the time, didn't run like the rest of her siblings. She just stood still and covered her eyes. When Papa Sebastiano saw her, he asked her what she was doing standing there with her hands over her eyes.

She answered, "Papa, if I don't see you, then you can't see me!"

She so thoroughly charmed him that he started to laugh and forgot his anger.

Surrounded by all this goodness, love and attention, the desire for my Papa Giulio was still always with me.

1922–1923

Mamma Vincenza, Maria Marzia;
standing is Domenico (Mimi); seated in front is Francesco (Ciccillo)

King Victor Emmanuel III and Mussolini

Neapolitan-born, King Victor Emmanuel III was loved and admired by the people of Santa Nicola and greatly respected by all Italians. They affectionately called him their "Little King." Benito Mussolini formed the Fascist Party and became prime minister in October 1922. He started setting up schools and getting the farm children off the farms and educated.

In town, every household was given a book with the fascist insignia on the front cover. The insignia was a gathering of sticks signifying unity: "All as one, equally shared."

Every week Mamma Raffaela prepared sauce for our Sunday dinner. I stood on a chair at three years old and helped her stir it. She also prepared braciole and sometimes added a browned piece of pork, lamb or even a chicken leg to the sauce. Papa Sebastiano prepared a jug with peaches and wine for dessert.

Papa Sebastiano had a mustache. When the meal ended he gave each child a piece of peach that had soaked in the wine. Then he attempted a sip of wine. He pretended there was a fly in the wine so we wouldn't ask for any more peaches, not that he would have denied us had we asked. But after he made believe the fly was caught in his mustache and he chased it away, we just didn't ask. It worked; we all believed him! The adults just laughed at his joking. We children took him very seriously. Not one of us asked for another piece of peach. Again, he was a wise man, not fully introducing us to wine. He only had it around for Sunday dinners.

Once, when I was three years old, Mamma told me to taste something at dinner. I responded, "I have no fork!"

Mamma offered hers, saying, "Here, use mine."

With a strong look of indignation on my face I replied, "Can't eat, *u scifato!*" How dare my Mamma think that I would use a fork that wasn't clean!

The adults were all astonished that I found even the suggestion of using my mother's fork repulsive. They said, "Just listen to her, spoken like a true Maiello!" They laughed, surprised that at three years old I'd spoken like that. But I couldn't use a dirty fork, even if it was my own Mamma's.

The Maiello family was noted for their habit of not sharing utensils or cups. They were way ahead of their time in cleanliness and aware of germs.

Papa Sebastiano loved home-cooked beans and could eat them prepared any way, five days a week. He liked them plain over cut up bread, topped with salt, pepper, a dash of oregano, olive oil and a few slices of raw onion. He also enjoyed them as *pasta fagioli*, with either red or white sauce, with rice or escarole, or as a cold salad made with lemon and olive oil. (Mamma Vincenza came to hate beans with a passion from overexposure to them!) These dishes were called *primo piatto*. *Secondo piatto* consisted of meat or chicken with assorted vegetables, then fresh fruit. Meals ended with black espresso coffee. How it came to be called demitasse, I'll never know.

For breakfast every morning the Veccia family had espresso and biscotti. We children put sugar in our coffee. The adults used a drop of anisette. The Maiello children were given bread for breakfast, which they dunked in wine. Only poor people used chicory root as a substitute for their coffee.

Hot chocolate was used only as a special breakfast treat, given to us on the morning of our saint's holy name day. The celebration of holy name days took precedence over birthday celebrations. Only once a year, we were served this delicious hot chocolate with two cookies when we first awakened, and we looked forward to it with great anticipation.

The farmers came early in the morning and brought their milk cows into town with full udders. They tied them up on the wrought iron gates in front of the church and milked them to sell the milk, which was warm, foamy and delicious.

When she saw the farmer arrive, Mamma sent us out to get some milk for ourselves. The farmer had only one cup with him, and everyone took turns drinking the milk, using that same aluminum cup with a handle.

Mamma always made sure that I had my own cup to use from the house (so I wouldn't get that sick *scifato* feeling in my stomach!).

THE GROCERY STORE

1924

Mamma took great pride in running the grocery store. The store was the one given to her by Papa Sebastiano when she was fourteen years old. When she stayed home during the five years that Papa was still in Italy, her younger sisters, Filomena and Carolina, and her brother Nicola helped her papa in the store.

She was so conscientious about showing a profit to please her Papa that she worked seven days a week. She sold everything the town needed, including fresh-baked bread that her brother Rocco baked every night in his bakery. She also sold all different types of pasta, olive oil, beans, cheeses and dry goods. The store itself had wall units with glass enclosures and the dry goods were scooped out with a large scoop, measured and sold.

Papa Sebastiano built a wooden form that created bags out of paper. Once formed, they were glued on the bottom. Everyone helped glue the bags, even the children. We were always making bags. Customers took their purchases home either in these bags or in the little red kerchiefs that they brought with them. Some of the townspeople refused the bags we made; they wanted true weight on the scale!

Mamma also kept the ledger straight, balanced the books and noted all monies owed to them and payments made. We knew the rules: we were never forbidden, but we just didn't take a piece of candy from the jar on the counter without paying for it, so strong was her desire to please her Papa Sebastiano and show a profit. She even charged her own Mamma and sisters. This became the family's private joke. She was teased about it and we all laughed together.

Zio Rocco Veccia

Mamma's big brother was our Zio Rocco. Like his Papa, he was also greatly respected and loved by the townspeople. The bond between Mamma and her brother was very strong. They made all the decisions that concerned the family, and the family lovingly obeyed them.

For Rocco's wedding to Michela, his parents gave him a large brass bed. He was also given the bread store and bakery to run, because Papa Sebastiano felt that a married man needed his own business. He moved back to the house with the bakery where his parents had once lived and settled with his wife. Rocco and Michela had six children. Due to Zio Rocco's involvement in the Church of Santa Nicola, the family donated many pews, and their names are still found there on the pews.

Zio Rocco spent his nights at the bakery so that the townspeople would have their morning bread. We children had our evening meal with Nonna Raffaela and Papa Sebastiano. Mamma's plate was usually brought to her in the store. She ate as she continued to work. Papa Sebastiano always wanted her to close the store during the meal, but she didn't want the townspeople to do without something they needed.

After our meal, and while Mamma was still working, Papa Sebastiano occasionally left us to join the men in the Circle of Santa Nicola if he had something to discuss with them.

Zio Rocco took all of us children into the bakery for a special evening treat made of fresh hot bread from the oven. He took a loaf, slit it open and drizzled olive oil on it. Then he opened a big jar of anchovies preserved in oil and spread them on the bread, closed the large hero sandwich and cut slices for everyone. After our snack, Zio Rocco retired for the evening and we went to meet Mamma in the store.

If Papa Sebastiano hadn't yet returned from the Circle, Mamma Raffaela sent one of us to call for him. We would go but never hung around there were all men there.

Sometimes, Zia Carolina, Zia Filomena and Zio Nicola sat with us around the brazier in the store and listened to ghost stories.

Mamma generally closed the grocery store at about 8:00 p.m. Then, my brothers and I helped her collect water needed for the bakery from the *acqua de serena* fountain. This was the purest water in town, piped in from the mountains. We filled a barrel from the fountain and then pushed it slowly on four wheels to the bakery. Mamma mixed the dough for her brother Rocco, preparing it for his nightly job, and finally we all headed to bed.

We walked home quickly, around the bend and the public fountain on the Via Santa Croce, to our bedroom in the palazzo. When we arrived we ran up the stone stairs and went straight to bed to say our prayers and hear another ghost story from Mamma.

When we were safely tucked under the sheets, Mamma told us her favorite story, called "The Golden Boot."

The Golden Boot

There once was a woman who wore a golden boot. She was a widow who had three daughters and raised them alone. Then she died and was buried. The three girls were starving to death, so the two older girls went to the cemetery and dug up their mother's body. When they went to pull off the golden boot the leg came off with it! They brought the leg home and put it under the youngest sister's bed, not telling her what they did.

The first night, their dead mother came and sang as she thumped up the stairs with one leg. THUMP! "I made the first step." THUMP! "I made the second step." THUMP! "I made the third step." But then she left because she had to go back to the cemetery when the clock struck midnight.

The second night, she came again, singing as she thumped up the stairs with one leg, THUMP! "I made the first step." THUMP! "I made the second step." THUMP! "I made the third step." THUMP! "I made the fourth step." But again she had to leave because the clock was striking midnight.

On the third night, the two older sisters were very scared, and having heard their mother's two previous attempts to get her leg back, went to sleep in another room. They left their youngest sister alone in their bedroom. They heard their mother coming.

Again she sang as she thumped up the stairs with one leg. THUMP! "I made the first step." THUMP! "I made the second step." THUMP! "I made the third step." THUMP! "I made the fourth step." THUMP! "I made the fifth step." THUMP! "I made the LAST STEP!" With two previous nights of practice she made it to the top of the staircase, and knowing where her leg was hidden, she went right to it.

The youngest sister, alone in the room, woke up, saw her mother and said, "Mamma, Mamma I'm so glad you are here. But, Mamma, what happened to your beautiful face?"

The mother replied, "THE WORMS ATE IT!"

Then the little girl asked, "Mamma, what happened to your beautiful eyes?"

The mother replied, "THE WORMS ATE THEM!"

Finally the little girl noticed the missing leg and said, "Mamma, what happened to your leg?"

In a very deep voice the Mamma said, "GIVE ME MY LEG!" Then she took it and went back to her grave.

And the little girl died of fright!

Mamma finished her story and went to the sitting room to do some sewing before she went to bed. I hid under the sheet until I fell asleep!

Mamma's Pet Names for Her Children

Francesco, or "Ciccillo" as she called him, was sickly as a young child, but brilliant. Mamma geared him toward becoming a scholar. He attended local school and went on with his studies at the high school in Caserta, near the Palazzo Reale. He aimed toward being a marine in the navy. He also studied with a private tutor.

Domenico, or "Mimi" as she called him, was smart, strong and healthy. He attended school in Santa Nicola and also worked with Zio Rocco in the bakery. Mimi complained that he would become a hunchback from carrying all the heavy loaves of bread each day. He always commented about "our brother the studente" as he worked. He delivered the bread, kept an eye on Zio Rocco's children, and went to the garden to collect chicken eggs for Zia Michela. This was a lot of responsibility for a young boy. Sometimes, Mamma took him away from the bakery for a while to give him a break.

Ciccillo always climbed out the window and ran downstairs to look for Mimi so they could play marbles and he could hide from the tutor. But the tutor always went to the store and complained to Mamma. Ciccillo never got away with it; they found him every time.

My nickname was "Marziella," which meant little Marzia, after my Nonna Marzia. I refused to answer to it. I made believe I didn't hear them calling me, never answered back and just walked away.

Zia Carolina Veccia

During the winter, after dinner and our snack with Zio Rocco, Mamma's sister Carolina's husband lit the brazier in the grocery store and told us ghost stories while Zia Carolina put the baby to bed for the evening.

Ciccillo, Mimi and I sat with Carolina's two sons, huddled around the brazier and hoping the small fire would ward off the coolness in the air. We all sat in wide-eyed wonderment as he spun his tales, while Mamma straightened out the store and prepared to close up for the night.

Antonio, or "Zio Totonno" as we children called him, was a tall, handsome man and a wonderful storyteller who also enchanted us with the Tales from the Arabian Nights.

Zio Totonno was the best man that I ever came across. He was a wood carver and worked very hard, carving large tree trunks into hand tools for farmers to thresh the wheat from the chaff. Yet he was always so pleasant to all the children that constantly hung around him, even while he worked. We all loved him.

Papa Sebastiano initially had been against the marriage of his daughter, Carolina, to Antonio Venerio. Antonio's mother had a bad reputation in town. When Antonio heard of his intended father-in-law's opposition, he went to the Veccias and said, "Show me a hill of garbage and a rose will come out of it!" And true to his word, he was a perfect rose, loved by all to the day he died.

I always said to myself that if I ever grew up and got married, I wanted a husband just like him.

Ciccillo (Francesco), Maria Marzia, & Mimi (Domenico)

Papa Sebastiano's Favorite Story

Sometimes, Papa Sebastiano told his favorite story as we sat around the brazier with Zio Nicola, our youngest uncle. It was the story of Death.

Death was once a very young and beautiful woman. She got her orders from God, and a daily list of names of the souls she was supposed to take each day on her journey.

One day she traveled to the next name on the list. She went to a household where she was to take the father of five children. He was a very sick man, and dying.

His wife begged Death, "Please do not take him away. How will we eat if you take our breadwinner away? We will all starve!"

Death felt sorry for the family and didn't take the man. She went on to the next name on the list. Much later, when she returned to God, she explained that she hadn't had the heart to take this one man.

God took Death by the hand to a spot in the woods and lifted a large rock to show her some very big, fat worms under it.

God said, "Look at all these worms. Who takes care of them? See how fine and healthy they are, yet they have no father."

Then, He said, "I am always at the helm; you took too much upon yourself. The decision was not yours to make. For disobeying my commands you will roam in all kinds of weather. The elements will destroy your youth and beauty, you will become old and ugly in your travels."

This story made a big impression on me. Since Papa Sebastiano had told it, I reasoned it as truth he would never tell a lie. I was awed by him and marveled that he knew such things.

Zia Filomena Veccia

Mamma's other sister, Filomena, married a sickly-looking man from Caserta Vecchio. Filomena's husband died within a year. His mother beat Filomena; she blamed her for her son's death. Papa Sebastiano took Filomena back home. She returned to work in the grocery store with Mamma.

After a while, Filomena met a handsome trapper in the store, by the name of Pasquale Izzo. He was from the Town of Paoliso, which is in the Province of Benevento (the area where, it was rumored, all the witches came from).

Pasquale fell in love with Filomena and courted her. He stated that he was a widower who was left with three children to raise.

Mamma was against the marriage because her sister Filomena had no patience with children. To try to win over and please Mamma, Pasquale gave her a beautiful fox wrap, and a baby fox wrap for me.

The courtship continued and they eventually married. They settled down with his three children in his house in Paoliso.

A few months after their marriage, his ex-sister-in-law arrived at their front door with his two remaining children. She presented them to Filomena and said, "Here are two more that are also yours."

He had five children, not three. His explanation was that he would never have found a wife if she knew he had that many kids.

Filomena took the children into their home, and she and her husband went on to produce five more together.

Zia Filomena and her husband introduced me to porcini mushrooms. His oldest daughter from his first marriage taught me how to look for them. When I stayed with them in Paoliso, we went up to a big mountain for a mushroom hunt. When we brought them home, my aunt would broil them in the coal stove. I can still remember the delicious taste of those broiled mushrooms.

Zio Pasquale continued to hunt and trap; that was his livelihood. I liked Zia Filomena, Zio Pasquale, and the children from his first marriage very much and spent a lot of time with them. We all got along so well together. Whenever I visited them I wondered if we would see a fox while we were mushroom hunting. And what about the witch stories that Mamma told when we went to bed at night? Witches came from Benevento. Would I see one while I was there?

The Strega and the Town of Benevento

Mamma loved to warn us about witches. She told us a village story: Once there was a husband and wife. The wife disappeared once a month, at night. She would stand naked by the window and recite as she anointed herself with oil, "With rain and wind I'm going to the walnut trees in Benevento!" Then she flew through the window and disappeared.

Month after month, her husband, pretending to be sleeping, watched her do this. One night he decided to follow her. He waited for her to leave and then went to the window, naked, anointed himself with oil and repeated her words; "With rain and wind I'm going to the walnut trees in Benevento."

Then he fell out the window and broke both his legs!

IN MY FATHER'S HOUSE

The Maiello Palazzo

Maiello Palazzo

Mamma had a large studio apartment in the Maiello house. The house was two stories high and had a large statue of Bacchus, the god of wine, on the roof. On the side of the house, facing the Via Santa Croce, was a small chapel. It was seldom used.

You walked into an alley off the Via Santa Croce to enter the double front doorway. This doorway was so large that a horse and buggy could enter through it. It was closed and locked every night with a large board placed against large hooks on the inside of the two doors.

When you passed through the doorway you entered a wonderful inner courtyard that was always filled with pots of flowers and shared by all the apartments in the house. There was an open staircase on the right, which led to an open verandah. The bedrooms were all off the verandah; our bedroom was at the top of the stairs.

There was a smaller, enclosed staircase on the left of the courtyard. It was private. The rooms close to this staircase, on the first floor, were for storage, stables, and access to the winepress room and the kitchen for the farm workers.

Nonna Maiello's private family kitchen was in the far corner on the first floor, along with a cold room and food storage area. Near the cold room were the stairs leading down to the wine cellar. The stairway had sixty steps just to reach the wine cellar! It was very scary to me. That cellar was also used to store fresh produce.

The vats for winemaking were so huge that we children played in them. My brother, Ciccillo, climbed up a ladder and cleaned the vats with sulfur when they were empty.

Just as you entered the courtyard through the front doors, there was a double-seated bathroom with cesspool on the right and a well to the left. The well had a stone washboard next to it, where family and tenants washed clothes together. The courtyard was strung with many clotheslines on laundry days.

We children loved to play in the rows of freshly washed clothes, but we were all afraid of the well.

The Well

Once, an old man fell into the well in the courtyard and died. From that day on, no one went near the well at night. They thought the old man's ghost haunted it, so it was used only during the day, to wash clothes and water the animals.

One day my brother, Mimi, was playing at the well. Mimi was five years old and platinum-haired.

From the balcony, Zia Ninella (Anna) saw something white fall into the well. She thought it was Mimi. She ran from the balcony down the stairs and across the courtyard to the well, screaming as she ran, "Mimi is in the well! Mimi is in the well!" When she got to the well, she was so overcome that she fainted.

I was in the courtyard and got very upset to hear her screaming and see her pass out.

When she screamed, everyone ran to the courtyard. Concerned, they tried to revive Zia Ninella, who was on the ground. Others, who came when they heard the screaming, were searching for Mimi, calling his name, checking doorways in the courtyard, looking all around for him. A few men were frantically pulling the rope on the bucket at the well.

Because of all the confusion, no one, including me, noticed Ciccillo, Mamma and Mimi standing together in the courtyard. Mamma was holding Mimi's hand.

Mamma kept repeating, "Mimi is here! Mimi is here!" No one listened to her.

When the men finally hoisted the bucket and pulled out a dead white dog, they knew that the real victim had been found.

Monk's Fat

The stone walls of the Maiello house had aged to a beautiful patina. In certain spots they actually shone with age. The town legend that was repeated to Ciccillo, Mimi and I, was that the building was once an ancient monastery, and monks were buried in the wall by the staircase.

They told us, "The shine on the wall is monk's fat oozing through it."

We all believed them. We were afraid to walk too close to the wall while ascending the staircase to the bedroom, for fear of monk's fat, while keeping an eye on the courtyard, terrified that we would see the ghost of the old man who died in the well!

We all ran, scared, up the stairs to our beds (Mamma, too), where we kept our eyes closed tight and the muslin sheets over our heads. Then we said our evening prayers and Mamma told us another ghost story! (I don't know how I was supposed to live through all of this.)

Visions

One time I walked in the courtyard late at night with Mamma and my two aunts, Zia Margarita and Zia Miluccia. It had gotten very late because we were in the kitchen baking for *Buona Pasqua*, the Easter holiday. And because it was so late and so dark outside, we were all frightened to walk through the courtyard to get to the bedrooms upstairs. We thought we would see the ghost of the old man who had died in the well.

As we approached the staircase, in fear I glanced over to the well. Instead of the ghost, I saw my friend, who lived in the palazzo, walking back and forth in front of the well wearing wooden shoes that were going click, click, click on the pavement.

Stunned to see her outside alone and unsupervised so late at night, I immediately stopped and said, "Look! There's Antonietta walking over there, and just what is she doing out alone at midnight?"

My aunts glanced over to the well, put their hands over my mouth and quickly dragged me by the arms up the stairs, past the wall of monk's fat, straight to Mamma's bedroom. They marched across the verandah into Nonna Marzia's room and told her what I had said. Nonna Marzia came to me and, with a very stern voice, said, "What you saw tonight, the others did not see. Don't tell the townspeople what you saw, because we will never have another tenant!"

That night my brothers were already asleep when I went to bed. After my prayers, Mamma told me the story of *Fantasima*, a spirit that lived in the well. When she came out at night she got taller and taller until, like a huge cloud, she reached the sky. She looked for children to steal!

My imagination was strong and I had to walk the verandah whenever I went to see Nonna Marzia. After that story, every time I passed the well I ran about a hundred miles an hour, out of fear.

Obeying Nonna Maiello

Nonna Marzia often sent me down to the wine cellar to get fresh melons that were stored there. In the wine cellar was also the same well where the old man died. I was terrified I might see his ghost there, too. Afraid and all alone, I stood at the top of the stairs. I hesitated, trying to gain courage, as I looked all the way down sixty steps to see the bottom. I was afraid to go but I would never think of refusing Nonna. Even in my fear I didn't want to displease her, so I ran down the steps, grabbed a melon and ran back up those steps scared out of my wits.

The Cold-Room

By the staircase to the cellar was the cold-room. It was always filled with big jugs of vinegar peppers, olives and all different kinds of cheeses.

Mamma loved to eat all these things, especially with a nice piece of bread fresh from the oven. She thought that everything was so delicious.

Sometimes, Nonna Marzia teased my Mamma. She said, "I think a little mouse got into that room and did quite a job."

Mamma was always embarrassed and her cheeks turned red as a beet.

MAMMA GIONA

Vincenza

Mamma had a physical strength and stamina that was just unbelievable. Her mental determination and perseverance always got the job done. She was always compassionate and caring. She worked tirelessly at her store, with her brother Rocco for his bakery, or to help anyone who ever asked for help.

Whenever we walked anywhere together, she wore her big mantle draped around her shoulders. My brothers walked on either side of her holding her arms, which left me to stumble along in front of them, sometimes tripping Mamma. She'd laughingly say, "Maria, stop tripping me!" Our love for each other was so great that we needed to be touching each other constantly. We were all so very close, and we were so important to her. Our attachment to her was as boundless as our love for her.

She taught us about life by telling us stories or reciting quotations. The stories could be religious in nature, or about witches, ghosts or folklore. The quotations she repeated were simple, yet thought-provoking words to allow reflection time in any given situation, or just plain observations on the human condition. She repeated these stories over and over so that we would remember them and learn their lessons.

The religious stories Mamma told us were either biblical or the legends and folklore surrounding the holy saints. The saints' holy name days were honored.

St. Anthony was a beloved saint of the area. He was celebrated on June 13th. You were to pray to him to help you find lost things.

St. Nicholas, our town's namesake, was always depicted standing by a barrel and holding up three fingers.

His story was that as a young man, he was hungry and went to an inn to get something to eat. He asked the innkeeper what he had to offer and the innkeeper offered him delicious fresh tuna that was just prepared the day before.

Nicholas just knew that there was something wrong about the place, so he went over to a barrel in the inn, said a prayer and held up three fingers. Three young boys came out of the barrel. The innkeeper had killed the children and chopped them up the day before. He had been serving them as fresh tuna!

Miraculously, the children lived again. St. Nicholas had saved them.

We had a feast in his honor every year in our little town.

Mamma and her family instilled in us that we should always be on time, never take a penny that didn't belong to us, and never tell a lie. Mamma told us that a lie had a hundred legs but couldn't stand up. For years I visualized a fat worm with many legs trying to stand. Mamma certainly knew how to get her point across.

She also told us not to put all grasses into one bundle, because you might get some bad grass in it along with the good. She meant that we should not judge everything the same, in that there are always exceptions to the rules.

But for the life of me, I could never figure out what possessed Mamma to tell us those ghost stories at bedtime. The pattern of our lives would set the mood. We'd close the grocery store and walk home past Zio Rocco's house, where Mamma once saw *Mazzamauriello*, enter the palazzo at night, with the well we feared in the courtyard, run past the wall of monk's fat on the staircase, and then go to bed. (Mamma repeated the story of Mazzamauriello so often that I became afraid of little men.)

In bed, we prayed for all our relatives, mentioning the living and the dead by name, and then Mamma told us a ghost story that left us shaking and hiding under the sheets! And how she loved singing the dead mother's part in the "Golden Boot" story, she took such great delight in telling it. I don't know if these stories were supposed to put us to sleep at night or scare us to death, but somehow we survived.

Curse of the Devil, or The Legend of St. Giuliano

Every night Mamma told us a different story. This one, which she sang to us, was very sad. She also sang it while she worked on the sewing machine.

There was a young couple who had only one child, a son. They loved him so much. They took him to a soothsayer who told them that their son would kill his parents when he was an adult. As much as they loved him, they abandoned him and went far, far away.

Twenty years later, the couple thought they should check on their son and wondered what kind of man he'd grown to be. They returned to their old town, found their son's house, went there and met his wife. She said that he had his own business and they were doing quite well. She invited them in, saying that their son would be so happy to see them. She explained that he was still at work and told the couple to go upstairs to rest before he arrived home. They thanked her and retired to the bedroom.

Meanwhile, evil suddenly got into their son at work. He felt that his wife was in bed with another man. He decided to go home and went into his house the back way. He entered into his bedroom and killed the man and woman that he found in his bed. Then he went downstairs and was stunned to find his wife in the kitchen.

His wife just couldn't wait to tell him of the surprise that she had waiting for him. His remorse was so terrible that he stabbed himself to death.

How he managed to become a saint I'll never understand!

Mamma wanted us to learn how to analyze things before jumping into them, so we would not be so impulsive, and think first before acting. So another night, another story.

Save the Fury of the Night for the Morning

There was a married man who left his wife and son and went away for many years. He finally became so lonely for his family that he decided to return home. He first went to a fortuneteller, who told him, "Save the fury of the night for the morning."

When he returned to his hometown, instead of going to his old house he rented a room across from it and watched it from the window. Through the front window of his old house, he saw his wife kissing a strange man. When he saw this happen, he got very angry. Even after all those years away from home he was still jealous! He was fuming about what he saw, but decided to try to get some sleep. Despite his anger, he remembered the fortuneteller saying, "Save the fury of the night for the morning." He decided that he would investigate further in the morning.

The next morning he went throughout the town, asking about his wife. Everyone told him what a wonderful woman she was. Every person he asked told him that she was a very holy woman and very involved in the church. One man told him about how proud she was of her son, who, just the previous day, had been ordained as a priest.

So the man that he'd seen his wife kissing the previous day was their son, the priest. It was good that he had saved his fury of the night for the morning.

He returned home filled with love and pride.

If he had taken action during his anger and jealousy, without finding out the truth, this story might have ended just as tragically as the legend of St. Giuliano.

Another Story: The Soothsayer

There was a young man who decided to travel. He went to a soothsayer and paid him some good denari for advice. The soothsayer told him three things:

1. Don't change the old road for the new.
2. Never tell your wife everything; hold back some things.
3. Never make friends with a policeman.

He listened to the soothsayer's advice about not changing the old road for the new and went home to test out the rest of the advice that he had paid good denari for. When he got home he told his wife, "I just killed a man. Please keep it a secret and tell no one."

His wife couldn't wait to tell their best friend, a policeman, who promptly came over and arrested him and threw him into jail.

In the jailhouse, the man explained that they couldn't hold him because there was no body of evidence. He said that he was just testing the advice that he got from the soothsayer that he had paid good denari for.

And to show us how strong is a mother's love she told us the story of—

'A Mother's Love'

A son kills his mamma. He carries her heart, walking to the cemetery. He trips, but catches himself before he falls.

He hears his mamma's voice ask, "Did you hurt yourself, my dear son?"

To Catch a Witch, or Get Caught By One

Mamma always said, to catch a witch you should attach a string to half a barrel laid on its side, light a candle in the barrel and wait for the witch to be attracted by the candlelight. (She explained that witches were always drawn to fire, because they were fascinated by it.) When you see the witch going into the barrel toward the lighted candle, you pull the string very quickly to trap the witch inside.

Ciccillo and Mimi tried this out but they never found any witches in the overturned barrel the next morning.

Midnight Relief

There once was a man who had to visit the outhouse in the middle of the night. When he went outside he heard singing, and as he walked toward the outhouse he saw a coven of witches dancing and chanting in a circle around a burning fire in a meadow near the woods. Half-asleep and not quick enough to hide from them, he was caught.

The witches pulled him into the center of their circle and continued to chant and dance around him. They wouldn't make an opening for his escape and they danced on and on for hours.

Unable to flee, and with every passing minute even more desperate to use the outhouse, he joined in their dance and chanted to their tune with his own words: "I'll never go to the outhouse in the middle of the night again. I'll never go to the outhouse in the middle of the night again. I'll never go to the outhouse in the middle of the night again."

On and on they all chanted and danced for hours.

Perhaps he was just having a bad dream or had drunk too much wine.

Werewolves

Every young girl in town was warned very strongly to never become pregnant around the end of March after they married. According to folklore, if you were impregnated in late March and your child was born at midnight on Christmas Eve, the baby would be born a werewolf.

Story of the Werewolf

Once there was a newlywed couple. They loved each other very much. They settled into their house after the wedding ceremony. After a few weeks went by, one night the husband told the wife that he had to go out for a while.

He said, "When I return home, whatever you do, don't open the door for me until I have knocked on the door the third time."

The wife, being a new bride, didn't understand, but told her husband she would follow his wishes. He left home in the evening.

Many hours went by; the wife started to worry about her husband. More hours passed and she longed for him to return home. Finally she heard him at the door, but it was so late and she was so anxious to see him that she didn't heed his warning to wait for the third knock on the door.

When she heard the first knock she ran to the door to open it for him. When she opened the door she saw a werewolf. He came into the house and slashed her to death.

Only when his transformation finally took place with the sunrise and he was once again a man did he realize what he had done.

'BUON NATALE' AND 'BUONA PASQUA'

'Buon Natale' and The 'Epifania'

On Christmas Eve every house in town had a *crèche* set up. Zio Rocco used his big bread table to serve the whole family a dinner of homemade pasta with *putanesca* sauce and eggplant parmigiana, among other dishes.

The *putanesca* was made with tomatoes, black olives, capers, garlic and anchovies, and was delicious. Before Zia Filomena married Zio Pasquale the trapper, she was the person who served dinner. She filled each dish by bringing the long strands of spaghetti high up into the air so all the goodies fell off into the big serving bowl. Then she served herself last and took all the goodies. Everyone laughed about it; she thought we didn't know what she was doing!

The mountain people, called "The *Pastori*," came from their Town of Abruzzi only once a year with their musical instruments called *zambogna*. They wore heavy socks and dressed in the traditional garments of mountain people from their area. They traveled throughout the region during the holiday season, playing in different towns.

The *Pastori* played "*Pastorale Della Notte Santa*" (Pastoral of the Holy Night) or "*Tu Scendi Dalle Stelle*" (You Come from the Stars), which was the "*Oh, Bambino Mio Divino*" song.

They walked the streets and came into your house and played the *zambogna* by your *crèche*. It was very solemn, like a prayer, and when they finished, Papa Sebastiano, tipped them in appreciation. Everyone in town would take care of the *Pastori* in this way.

After the music and dinner we attended mass.

On the *Epifania* we children hung our stockings on the bedpost at night. In the morning we found little gifts of walnuts or oranges in them.

La Befana was the Italian equivalent of Santa Claus. On the *Epifania*, January 6th, *La Befana* came to put sweets or small gifts in your stocking, but only if you had behaved in the past year. If you were a bad child, *La Befana* left only a piece of coal or a switch. And sometimes, if you were naughty, she might come just to steal you away.

La Befana was a little old witch-woman who flew around on a broom. She used her broom to fly down the chimney to deliver her presents.

According to her legend, the Three Wise Men stopped at her house to ask for directions on their way to Bethlehem to see the Christ child. They asked her to come along with them, but she told them that she was much too busy sweeping and sent them away.

After the Wise Men left, *La Befana* was filled with remorse and tried to follow them. She couldn't catch them and has been flying around Italy ever since, looking for the Christ child. She became old and very wrinkled after many years of fighting the elements in her travels.

Each year she leaves presents at the house of every child, just in case one of them is the Christ child.

'Buona Pasqua'

Carnevale was the last night before the start of the Lenten season, or the last day of eating meat. Fasting for lent consisted of eating only watermelon and bread. Eggs were stored in cold rooms for weeks in advance of the holiday, in preparation for the traditional meat pies and wheat pies that were baked.

The forty days of lent were to honor the passion and death of Christ. They were the most solemn time of year. Easter morning was a celebration of Christ's resurrection.

Once a year, before Easter week, all the families in town put large basins of water in their courtyards. We were told to look into the water to see the reflection of Salome and her mother, Herodias.

As we looked into the basin, the adults recited, "They were to be seen riding on a beam of fire for all eternity. Their punishment for the beheading of John the Baptist."

We looked and looked into the large basin of water. Needless to say, no one ever saw the reflections, but it gave us a chance to stay up late at night, which we all loved.

During Easter week, the family packed up a picnic lunch and walked to the Palazzo Reale, in the city of Caserta. We brought with us all the home-baked goodies the women had prepared for the holiday. Only once a year, at Easter, were the grounds of the Palazzo opened to the public.

We sat on the grass during these picnics, overwhelmed by the beauty surrounding us. Someone eventually told the story of Luigi Vanvitelli, the builder, who was blinded by the Bourbon King Carlo so he couldn't create another Palazzo Reale. There were lovely gardens with statues and waterfalls. We spent the day relaxing and enjoying all the home-baked specialties. At the end of the day we walked back home across the railroad tracks to Santa Nicola.

AT FOUR YEARS OLD

Maria Marzia, four years old

Convent School

Sometimes Mount Vesuvius rumbled and the ground shook. Everyone was afraid. But life wasn't all the terror of Vesuvius. I remember walking through fields of poppies. Of course I should have been in school at the time, but I was young and needed to see the poppies. I reveled in their beauty and enjoyed their surroundings. I saw them after lunch instead of returning to school. There was also the lovely warm weather, and all the other flowers and the sun, "*O Sole Mio*!" This was my season in the sun; I felt no guilt at all in missing school.

I was sent to a convent school that was located right next to the church. Mamma saw the school across the street from her store and felt confident with me so close by.

When I was in first grade, my teacher, the nun, had the lesson for the day on the blackboard. She drilled me on numbers one through ten. She pointed to the blackboard with her ruler and if I answered wrong, she hit my hands with the ruler.

I was only four years old and no one had ever hit me. I was so insulted!

So my afternoon excursions to the poppy fields and my love of nature were my solace and protection. I felt safe and not threatened there, and closer to God.

Every Time I Went to the Poppy Fields

I traveled through huge towering oak trees that were so beautiful and made an archway with their branches and leaves. Then, to get to the fields, I crossed a stream where the cypress trees grew. Every time I crossed the stream I fell in and got drenched. Then I had to dry my shoes, socks and dress in the hot sun so I wouldn't get into trouble when I returned home. But I never got into trouble because the grownups never knew I went there.

The stream was past a shortcut I used, near Nonna Maiello's house, and came after a pond. The shortcut was an alleyway a few houses down from Nonna's, and it was very dirty. The alley wasn't often used for walking because it was mostly a convenience when people had to relieve themselves and couldn't find a bathroom. I loved using this alley to get to my fields of poppies and flowers when they bloomed in the spring. And I still hadn't told Mamma the nun hit me. Through the alleyway, on the right, was the pond, which was sometimes extra muddy when it rained. It was very dangerous to get too close.

One time, on my way to the poppy fields, I went too close and got stuck in the mud. I started to sink. The mud kept sucking me down and there wasn't a soul to save me. I had such a difficult time, sinking deeper and deeper, but I finally struggled out of there. I was so scared that I ran shaking to the stream to clean up. I had mud up to my knees and had to rinse out my shoes and socks in the stream. When everything finally dried in the sun, I returned home the long way. The afternoon outing had been too much for me. That was the last time I ever used that shortcut!

A Different Education

Due to Mamma's involvement in her work in the grocery store, I spent a lot of time alone. I was left with many different relatives on extended visits and it exposed me to many experiences and people from many different walks of life. It also taught me to accept of all kinds of people and to make friends of all except nuns!

I never returned to convent school after I told Mamma the nun had hit me. I started attending public school in Santa Nicola.

But I never stopped escaping every spring to see my fields of poppies when they were in bloom.

1925

Feeding the Farm Workers

In the mornings I helped Zia Miluccia make all the beds and sweep the floors. After feeding them breakfast, Nonna Marzia sent the farm workers out in a large open truck. They were dropped off at different fields for their day's work. At noon, the family sent out food for them. Lunch consisted of large homemade rounds of bread, cheese, and a gallon of wine per section of field.

In the evenings the workers were picked up by the truck and brought back to the palazzo, where Zia Margarita fed them before they went home. Their children came to meet them after school and were also fed. Zia Margarita did all the cooking and everyone helped bake the bread. Dinner was cooked in large cauldrons and consisted of seasonal produce.

If broccoli or cauliflower was in season, the cauldron was filled with broccoli or cauliflower and macaroni. These soupy peasant dishes could also be a bean mixture, or pasta with cooked dried beans, chickpeas or green peas. Sometimes it was a dish of escarole and cooked dried beans. Each dish was its own recipe, started with olive oil and either onion or garlic. Then *proscuitto* or dried sausages were added, along with spices for flavoring.

I helped Zia Margarita serve the food and wine to the workers and their families, and also enjoyed dinner with them. After a day spent in the sweltering sun, the workers took their bowls and settled on the pavement to eat their meals in the late afternoon shade. Then the fun would start. There was always teasing and much laughter between them. When they finished their meals the families left for home, their long day's work done.

One farm worker was a woman whose husband had gone to America to work. While he was gone she became pregnant with another man's child and delivered their baby. She had no choice but to give this beautiful, perfect baby boy away. I felt so bad for her: I was scared and confused, I understood only that something was a sin.

Without warning, her husband returned home.

When I saw him in town, walking down the Via Santa Croce from the train station, I ran quickly to her home to tell her of his return. My heart went out to her and I felt she needed some advance warning. (I got excited whenever a man came home from America; I thought that someday it might be my Papa.)

Once her husband was home she soon became pregnant with his child. The baby was born deformed.

Cornbread

Zio Rocco baked mostly white bread in his bakery, but he also baked whole wheat. Zia Margarita baked white bread too, for the farm workers. The local farmers baked whole wheat and delicious cornbread.

The farmers knew that I loved their cornbread, so they waited for me to come and exchange my white bread for their cornbread. They specially baked me a little man made out of cornbread.

The farmers were always very kind to my brothers and me. This treatment of us as children goes under the heading of "Respect the dog for its owner." Our two families were held in very high esteem by the townspeople, and we were the little puppies who were the recipients of their respect, admiration and generosity. How blessed I was to have known so many wonderful people in my little hometown.

'Shola, Shola'

Santa Nicola La Strada was warm year-round, but somewhat cooler in the short winter months. The rains came during the month of April, when the crops had already been planted for the season.

During the long, hot summertime, some of the farm workers would get too hot in the sun during the day. They removed their pants to work. None of them wore underwear; they worked wearing only their long nightshirts.

If one of these men without pants had to climb to a loft to store hay, the old women yelled at them, "*Shola*! *Shola*!" as if they were shooing away a chicken. It seemed that the view the women were exposed to reminded them of a chicken.

The men grumbled and responded to the women with good-natured curses. They told the teasing women to go home to cook and clean. Everyone laughed. I thought that the farm workers were such fun.

The month of August was the time for ripe figs. These delicious fruits, plucked and eaten with a loaf of bread, were considered a major treat. Ciccillo, Mimi and I went through the alleyway by Zio Rocco's house and asked his neighbor for permission to eat the figs right off his tree. Once we had permission, we climbed up a ladder and sat on a branch of the tall tree to eat our fill. Not being very big and loving the fruit I ate even the unripe figs within my reach from my spot on the branch. Sometimes my mouth puckered with the unripe fruits, but that didn't stop me from filling up on them.

Oranges and big sweet lemons were picked and made into a refreshing late-night salad. Tomatoes were also harvested during August, and the tomato canning started. This was hard, time-consuming work. The jars had to be sterilized, the tomatoes needed to be cleaned and prepared, the filled jars had to be sealed correctly when they boiled, and the finished jars had to be stored.

It took days of hot sun to make tomato paste from tomatoes. They covered it with netting to keep the horseflies away. Salt was added as a preservative, and the paste had to be stirred daily. Each day fresh basil leaves were put on top to add flavor. It was brought in at night to the cold-room, only to return to the hot sun the following day, until finally, after many days it became tomato paste. The finished paste would keep for a long time and be used in the pasta and peasant dishes.

Fall harvest-time yielded potatoes, corn and apples. These were used mostly for animal feed, but the first picking of tender corn was cooked in a large cauldron and brought through town on a cart so people could taste the wonderful sweetness.

The farmer pushed the cart and yelled, "Hot corn, Hot corn!" You could buy an ear for a penny. The rest of the corn stayed on the stalks to ripen for animal feed.

Work

The palazzo was always busy with work to do, and everyone pitched in to help. The men also killed the yearly pig, which was made into *prosciutto*, salami and dry sausages.

It was so much work when the women made sausage and rendered the fat from the pig that even neighbors helped. When the work was done, they were given some of the meat. Then, when they killed their yearly pig and you helped them, they did the same for you. It needed many hands working together. When the sausages were made and half-dried, they were preserved in rendered pork fat. Then whatever was cooked started with sausage and the rendered fat. Delicious! The *prosciutto* was cured with pepper and salt and hung from a crossbeam near an oven.

I only watched the pig killing once; that was more than enough. Fighting and squealing all the way, the pig was dragged into a small pen by a few men. The awful squealing seemed to go on forever. Once they closed the pen, the butcher cut an artery in the pig's neck. The men caught the blood in a bucket to save it.

The pig squealed until finally it died. Then the butchering job started. The men always made sure to keep the meat from being contaminated by the guts and entrails. The intestines were saved, turned inside out and washed repeatedly. After each washing they were scraped. When they were finally clean they were preserved in salt and then used for the sausage casings. The blood that was saved in the bucket was made into a pudding called *sanguinaccio.*

Nonna Marzia's work kitchen was small and located near the wine storage area on the side of the cellar stairs opposite the family kitchen. This was where she cooked to feed the farm workers. The work kitchen had a bakery oven for making bread and a low wood-burning stove where two cauldrons were used to cook pasta and vegetable dishes. This kitchen was also where laundry soap was made. They mixed fire ashes with lye to make the soap.

The private family kitchen was very big. In addition to the large fireplace that was bordered with stone benches, there was a charcoal stove with six burners, a long work counter and a long wooden dining table with benches.

There were also three Singer sewing machines against the wall in the kitchen. Zia Ninella (Anna) did machine embroidery on them. Zia Margarita made shirts. Everyone used a sewing machine. I was already using one at four years old. Mamma was able to take the machine apart, oil it, and assemble it again. The sewing machines were also used to make men's shirts and undergarments and, of course, ladies' dresses. But many things were hand-sewn. Women's hands were always moving, always knitting socks.

The tenants in the house sometimes became like family. Whether it was a wedding, a death, or the birth of a new baby, everyone helped. If one of the tenants was pregnant, by the time the new baby arrived there were many beautiful handmade clothes all ready for the arrival. Hand needlework was very important, too.

Mamma did quite a lot of sewing. I loved the panties she made for herself: they were such a laugh because they were so ingenious. She created them by hand, with strings attached to the front panel at the waist that tied at the back, and strings on the back panel that tied in the front. So, when she had to go to the bathroom, only the back panel went down by untying the front strings, and the front panel stayed put. Mamma also made herself bras, which nobody used in those days, fashioned with beautiful white muslin with pretty white lace on the edges.

I worked on the sewing machines and also started my embroidery classes at that young age. I worked on delicate lacework and stitching as I became more skilled.

Papa's Brothers

Papa Giulio's brother, Zio Filippo, was the overseer in the fields. He fell in love with a married woman named Esperanza, whose husband had gone to America many years before Filippo met her. Filippo became the outcast in the family because he fathered two children with Esperanza out of wedlock, a boy, and a girl whom he named Marzia, after his Mamma.

Their daughter, my cousin Marzia, and I were secretly very close, but I never told my Nonna Marzia about my friendship with her.

Mamma was once sick with typhus, and Zio Filippo's woman was the only one to go near her to offer help. She gained Mamma's respect and admiration with these acts of kindness, and Mamma always spoke up for her. She said that women in such a predicament always had the biggest hearts of all.

Esperanza 's husband was gone for many years. He never returned to Italy and finally died in America. Zio Filippo married her when she received word that her husband died. The marriage changed his status with the family; he was welcomed back after many years and offered his entitled room in the Maiello palazzo. I was so happy for him. He was a good, kind and hardworking man.

Zio Domenico was a favorite in the family. He went to Brazil after Grandfather Francesco died, and lived a very good life. The family often spoke of him, and Mamma corresponded with him. He entertained them all with music and song. My brothers and I never met him, but we always heard stories about him and prayed for him, his wife, Serafina, and their family.

Zio Petrucci (Pietro) was another younger brother of Papa's. When Papa Giulio left for America, Zio Petrucci took me under his wing. When I went to visit, he took me by the hand and walked me to the cigar store to treat me to a chocolate bar. He never talked with the rest of the family, only me.

Oh, how I wished that it was my Papa that treated me to that candy bar. But even though I was young, I knew that Zio Petrucci, with his kindness to me, was trying to substitute for my papa.

Zio Petrucci eventually became the mechanic that his sister Angela Maria wanted him to be. He married and had three children. He and his family lived in a town called Colleferro. When his son was twenty-three years old, a hit-and-run driver killed him. Zio Petrucci and his wife never got over the tragedy. His wife went insane and spent the rest of her life in bed. Their two daughters took care of both their parents until they died.

Zio Eduardo was very tall and handsome, blue-eyed like all the other Maiellos. He married the woman he loved and when she died young, he raised their three daughters alone.

Lastly, Papa's baby brother, Francesco, was the child that Nonna Marzia was carrying when her husband Francesco died. My brother Ciccillo and our Zio Francesco were close in age and attended school together.

Zio Francesco eventually went on to become a town inspector and also a tour guide in the Palazzo Reale, a job that pleased his older sister, Angela Maria. He married a woman he was crazy about. They were so ridiculously in love that the townspeople murmured at their public displays of affection.

Papa's Sisters

Addolorada often came to visit us in Santa Nicola, from the Town of San Marco Ivangilista. With her husband away in America, she was very lonely. I understood her loss; she wanted to be with her family. She always brought her two sons when she visited us.

Zia Angela Maria lived in the City of Caserta. We visited quite often with her and Zio Michele, and I spent many nights staying overnight with them and cousin Pupetta.

Anna (Zia Ninella) was the greatest beauty in the family. When she was young she fell in love with a man from an influential family. He went to war in 1918. When he returned home he was paralyzed from the waist down. Although he loved Zia Ninella, he released her to find someone else. He explained that he could "never be a real husband to her."

Zia Ninella was heartbroken. She loved him dearly, but she honored his wishes and they parted. Although he had no use of his legs, he had full use of his arms, and was seen taking his small horse and *carrozzino* riding all over town. When he stopped the carriage at the Maiello house entrance, he gazed and then left. With his undiminished love for Zia Ninella he only wanted the best for her.

Since Zia Ninella was still young and considered a great beauty, the town butcher, Antonio Madonna, soon courted her. Zia Ninella married him. He was a good-looking man and very good to her. Antonio, or Totonno, as he was called, did very well with his butcher shop and rolled up thousand lire bundles of bills to throw in his safe.

Their two-room apartment in the Maiello house was beautiful. It was next to Nonna Marzia's bedroom. Their ceilings were covered with paintings embedded in marble tiles.

Their bedroom had a wardrobe that extended along the whole length of one wall. It was always filled with beautiful dresses and shoes to match, all lined up on the bottom shelf.

Zia Ninella and Totonno had two children, named Sophia and Pierino. They lived very well.

After Nonno Francesco died, Zia Ninella helped her mother, Nonna Marzia, when she struggled for money. Zia Ninella learned the combination of Totonno's safe and helped herself to a little bundle of money to give her mother. Totonno never counted his money so he never knew what she did.

Because her brother, Giulio, was in America, Zia Ninella also helped out her sister-in-law, Vincenza. She gave Mamma a steak a day for me. This was to build me up because I was so thin.

Zia Ninella was both kind and beautiful.

Papa's sister, Zia Margarita, was very sweet and pretty. I truly thought she was an angel, she had such great love and compassion in her heart. I was drawn to her by the goodness of her soul, and loved just being near her.

Zia Miluccia's name was actually Carmela. She was only five years old when Papa left for America in 1920. She begged her brother, Giulio, to never forget her. He never did.

THE TOWN OF CAIAZZO

Our Trips to Caiazzo

I loved to visit my great aunt, Zia Maria Antonia. She was my grandmother Raffaela's sister, and lived with her husband in the Town of Caiazzo. Caiazzo was a mountain town on the other side of the mountain from Caserta. I traveled with my grandparents, Mamma and brothers in a mule-drawn buggy. The trip was very long so we left very early in the morning.

We reached a point during the trip where we had to cross a small body of water by barge. The mule was usually so afraid of the water that it took three or four men just to pull him onto the barge. One time the mule was so scared that he panicked and ran and the men couldn't stop him. It took four men to keep him from running straight into the water. It was always exciting on these trips, and such fun.

Zia Maria Antonia was the exclusive weaver of linens for all the brides in Caiazzo. She worked on a loom so large that it filled a whole room in her apartment. She had beautiful linens in her home and a luxurious feather bed. Her bed, like all others in that town, was so high off the floor that she needed a chair and a step stool just to get into it. Some of the townspeople, had their coffins already made and waiting for them, stored under their own beds.

Zia Maria Antonia also performed all the local poultry operations, transforming roosters into capons. She took me with her and I watched as she held the young male chickens between her legs by their feet. With a knife she removed the cockscomb and quickly placed some loose feathers over the wound, to sterilize it, so she said. But it was really to keep the other chickens from pecking at the wound. Then, still holding the chicken, she made an incision near the tail, low on the belly, and scooped out the two testicles. Of course the chicken would be screaming by that time. She took her needle and thread and stitched them up. You can just imagine the noise they made.

In lieu of money for her services, she accepted fresh fruits and vegetables from the local farmers she worked for. There was always an abundance of fresh produce in the area. Her large work apron was filled by the time we arrived back at her house.

In the evening, after the capon work, she made dinner for me. Zia Maria Antonia took the cockscombs and testicles and fried them with onions in olive oil and served them to me.

I even commented, "They're so good!" What did I know about what I was eating?

Since I usually spent a great deal of time with her, Zia Maria Antonia took me to visit her sisters and friends. If they were bedridden, she washed them all over and made them smell nice. Most of the time they weren't even family, just friends. What lessons I got from this Good Samaritan.

Zia Maria Antonia would tell me the story of St. George Cavalier whenever I visited her. I loved the story so much that I never got tired of hearing it over and over again. So every night I stayed with her and after saying my prayers I was tucked into a feather bed to hear the Legend of St. George Cavalier.

In England in the olden times there lived a dragon. He was victimizing a town. The townspeople tried to keep him happy by sacrificing an offering of sheep to him. When that didn't make the dragon happy, the king decreed that human sacrifice was in order. Everyone was to take part, even members of the royal house. The sacrificial victim would be chosen by lot.

When the king's daughter's number was chosen, she had no choice but to go. Her father the king was despondent over his daughter's predicament, but being a noble and honorable king he had her taken out to be sacrificed to the dragon, per his own decree.

George, hearing of the princess' lot being chosen, ran to her rescue and bravely fought the ferocious fire-breathing dragon. It was a terrible battle, but George finally killed the monster. For George's bravery the king thanked him by knighting him. Grateful for his saving their beloved princess and the town, the whole kingdom converted to Christianity.

And I went to sleep dreaming of princesses and dragons.

'A Bella' and 'U Brutto'

When I visited Zia Maria Antonia in Caiazzo, I also visited one of her neighbors, a beautiful young lady who lived upstairs from her. The young lady's mother had arranged her marriage to a wealthy man who was deformed. He was all twisted on one side like a monster. When they married, "Beauty" was only twenty years old. He was in his thirties.

I made friends with the beautiful lady. She called to me to visit her whenever she knew that I was in town. I loved to visit her but never understood how she could tolerate a husband like him. I was six years old and cringed as I watched the man move toward his wife.

As I continued to visit them each time I went to Caiazzo, I came to realize that there was goodness in his heart. He was very kind to her and evidently crazy about her. And, after all, he really couldn't help what he was.

She never had children of her own. She offered to adopt me every time she saw my Mamma. She explained that I would live very well with them.

Mamma felt so badly for this beauty, and hated to tell her it could never be.

Zia Maria Antonia

On our trips to visit Zia Maria Antonia, Ciccillo and Mimi always came with us. We never left them behind. I never told them but they were my life. I couldn't live without them.

We all went for the visit and then my brothers left me to stay, sometimes for two weeks, sometimes for a month while they returned to Santa Nicola with Mamma, Papa Sebastiano and Mamma Raffaela. Someone eventually came to get me.

I dearly loved my Zia Maria Antonia, but after a while I got homesick for my brothers and family. She felt bad to see me go, but she understood. She never had any children of her own, but raised her stepchildren. They were not as close to her as we were.

She had a very strong attachment to me and also to my Mamma.

Roving Spirit

Zia Maria Antonia's neighbor had a son who was murdered. The poor woman was so despondent over her boy's death that she was inconsolable. She wanted to know who had killed her son and why.

Zia Maria Antonia sometimes heard a man's deep voice coming from their apartment, and it wasn't the voice of the neighbor's husband; it was much deeper and louder than his.

It was rumored that the woman had taken water from a bottle that had a roving spirit in it, and the spirit was speaking through this woman, ready to divulge the secret of her son's murderer.

When Zia Maria Antonia heard this loud booming voice, she ran into the hallway to listen at the outer wall of their apartment next door, at which point she heard the loud voice say, "I can't speak now, there's an ear at the door!"

Zia Maria Antonia ran back to her rooms completely terrified.

They never found out who killed the woman's son and I was shocked over the killing because they were such gentle people in that town.

1926–1927

Mussolini

By 1926, Mussolini had taken total control of the government and, with strong-arm tactics, rousing speeches, parades and uniformed schoolchildren, transformed the country into a single-party, totalitarian regime.

Schools had been set up under the dictator, and farm children were able to get an education. Santa Nicola had an empty building across from the public water fountain, and this was used to create our public grade school. Before that all grades were in the same class.

Mussolini finally made the trains run on time.

All Saints' Day, All Souls' Day

After the summers were over and the work on the farms slowed up, the weather got cooler, but never cold. As the days shortened, the holidays started.

November 1 was All Saints' Day, but the whole month of November was dedicated to the dead. The church was involved in memorials with masses said for deceased loved ones.

Behind the church, on the property along the Via San Marco, was an ancient wall, many centuries old. This wall was the back of an ancient crypt. Long ago it was the original church mausoleum where they buried the priests and monks. Once it was filled they used the cemetery grounds.

The local cemetery was in a different location. It was very old and very beautiful and would be awash with flowers in honor of All Saints' Day. The dead were buried in vaults, and each vault had a picture of the deceased loved one in front of it. A memorial marker with a name and face.

I loved walking to visit the cemetery each November; the flowers were always so beautiful. Our deceased relatives were buried in drawers in the mausoleum vaults.

Only people without families were buried in the ground.

At midnight on the eve of all Souls' Day, November 2, all the residents in town would hide in their homes. No one went outside.

According to folklore, at midnight on this day all the dead walked the earth once again. Thy walked two by two in procession, holding lighted candles in their hands. They traveled the streets throughout the town.

Every year the townspeople wondered if the story was truth or fiction, but their fear kept them inside their homes. No one risked seeing this ghoulish parade, so they hid.

One time, a wise guy decided to steal a candle to prove that the dead did indeed walk the earth on this one night a year. He waited until it was close to midnight, and then he went outside. Sure enough, he saw the procession that he had always heard about it was true!

He watched the dead, walking two by two, each holding a lighted candle. He stepped out into the street and grabbed one of the candles, his proof of just what he had done that evening. He took the candle and ran back to his house.

When he got home and looked at the candle in the light he saw to his horror that it wasn't a lighted candle, it was a finger! It was their fingers illuminating the way.

His terror was his payback for being a nosy wise guy.

Visiting Relatives

Each year as the Christmas season approached, our families visited each other to celebrate *Buon Natale*, the birth of Christ.

There were both Veccia and Maiello relatives living in Caserta. I loved going to visit them to see their crèche set up for the holiday.

The "*Casertanos*," as the people who lived in Caserta were called, were city folk and considered themselves the upper class of the area. They were usually well to do and generally better educated and better dressed than others in the surrounding areas. A Caserta woman just wouldn't be seen walking in town without wearing her hat and gloves.

The High School was located in Caserta, and young adults traveled to the city from neighboring towns to continue their education. This is where my brother Ciccillo attended school.

Most of Papa Sebastiano's sisters and brothers stayed in Caserta. Considering that they all grew up in an orphanage, they did quite well for themselves.

Papa Sebastiano's sister, Zia Carmela, owned a *gelati* store, another owned a bread store and another a *caffeteria.* (The cafes in Caserta served special coffee, *gelati* and pastries.)

One of Papa Sebastiano's brothers went to live in Foggia, Italy, and his brother, Zio David, went to America and settled in the Bronx, New York.

Mamma Raffaela had three sisters in the Town of Caiazzo. They all married and settled down in the immediate area, but some of her sisters' children went to America and settled in Connecticut.

I specially loved to stay with my Zia Angela Maria, her husband Michele and their daughter Pupetta. When I stayed overnight with them, we first enjoyed our dinner together and then we strolled, hand in hand, throughout the city. When we reached Zia Carmela Veccia's store we always stopped to visit her and experience the best-tasting *gelati* in the world.

What a treat—nowhere will you find better!

Ciccillo the Angel

Christmas Eve and putanesca sauce again! But Zia Filomena was in Benevento with Zio Pasquale and all their children, so I couldn't laugh at her serving our meal and keeping all the goodies for herself when she served dinner.

I was excited about the *Pastori* coming to play their *zambogna* for us and excited to see my brother Ciccillo perform. Ciccillo was the angel in the Christmas play each year. He had a speech to recite in which he portrayed the angel fighting with the devil.

The stage for the play was erected in the street. Ciccillo was rigged up with pulleys, and thrown out a window to hang over the crèche for his performance. He played the angel until he was fifteen years old, at which time he said, "Enough, already!"

The same men portrayed Jesus and Joseph each year. These men maintained beards throughout the year just for the play. Every year a beautiful woman was chosen to play Mary.

I hung a stocking on my bedpost and waited to see *La Befana* come on the *Epifania*, January 6th, but I fell asleep and missed her again.

I woke up to find walnuts and oranges in my stocking on the bedpost.

'Mulino' Amato

Papa Sebastiano had started out as a young man working as a guard in a wheat mill. He went on to establish a bread store in the same mill Town of Santa Maria. Then he and Mamma Raffaela moved from Caserta to the Town of Santa Nicola and opened another bread store and bakery. The grocery store that Mamma ran was set up for her so that she could have her own business.

Papa Sebastiano once took me with him to get supplies for the bakery at the mill in Santa Maria. We took the horse and buggy to the *Mulino* Amato, which was a spaghetti factory and wheat mill. When we arrived, Papa Sebastiano showed me the factory that made pasta. He ran the machines for me and I watched all different types of spaghetti coming out of them. I was so fascinated by it. I also saw all the racks set up for drying the spaghetti.

I found the whole day very interesting and just loved spending that time alone with my Papa Sebastiano.

One day, Papa Sebastiano was planning another business trip. He needed supplies from Santa Maria for his stores in Santa Nicola. Mamma had a horrible premonition that something terrible would happen that day. She pleaded with her Papa not to go. She cried and begged him to not go. She even pulled on his sleeve to try to keep him from going into his horse and buggy.

He finally said to her, "Why are you doing this to me? I have so much on my mind and need these supplies!" He got into the buggy and left for the mill. He spent the day purchasing flour there, loaded up the buggy and started for home.

On his way back he was stopped by a band of highwaymen. They beat Papa Sebastiano viciously, took all of his money and supplies and left him for dead.

The horse knew the way home; he had traveled the route so many times that he just took the carriage home with Papa Sebastiano in it.

Papa Sebastiano was so bruised that he could hardly move.

When the carriage got back to the house, Mamma ran out to meet it. She had worried all day about her Papa. When she saw the injured condition he was in, her heart was broken that he was so badly hurt. As she helped him into the house all he could say was that he was afraid to come home because he didn't want to hear her scolding him for not listening to her that morning.

From that day on, Mamma could never tell this story without tears flowing from her eyes; it upset her so much.

Passion Play

Between the towns of Santa Nicola and San Benedetto was a sports arena called *Fore Torno*. It was used for soccer games and horse racing.

During the Lenten season, when I was seven years old, they were showing a passion play in the rotunda at *Fore Torno*. It was a movie, and I had never seen the story of Jesus in movie form before so I went with neighbors to see it. Because there were so many people in the rotunda to view the film, the neighbors who brought me left without me after seeing it.

I continued watching the film, which they kept repeating over and over. When they stopped running the film it was late at night. I had to walk home five blocks alone. I wasn't missed by the adults because both sides of the family thought that the other side had me.

When I arrived home I found the grocery store all locked up for the night. I threw rocks at the upstairs windows until finally Mamma Raffaela and Mamma opened the door. They had ten fits when they realized what had happened, but the next morning all was forgotten.

I wondered why I was never hit or punished. Something terrible could have happened to me that night all alone. But it didn't. My guardian angel sure took very good care of me!

Palazzo Santoro

In Santa Nicola was the ancient house called Palazzo Santoro. It was across the street from Zio Rocco's house and bakery on the Via Santa Croce. The only family resident was Signore Santoro. He had a sister who visited him occasionally, traveling with a small horse and *carrozzino.*

Signore Santoro had married as a young man but the union produced no children. Then his wife left him. He lived alone in this big house, with a house chef and his wife the housekeeper, and their children.

The family resident aged along with his belongings with no one to carry on the family name. The furnishings were elaborate, with fine furniture collected from a distant era, and draperies and linens from floor to floor. The attic contained antiquities from bygone days. There was a small chapel right in the palazzo. The priest went there every Sunday to say mass for the residents.

Signore Santoro could be seen riding throughout town in his small horse and *carrozzino*, but most of his time was spent alone in the house. He had the bearing of nobility and the pallor of inbreeding about him.

On the grounds in the garden of the Palazzo Santoro was where Zio Totonno, Zia Carolina's husband, (my favorite uncle, so good to all of the children) had his wood carving shop set up.

One time my brothers decided to make me a concrete dollhouse. They mixed the cement and built the dollhouse three feet high and one and a half feet square. Before the concrete dried, they had me place a rod into it so that once it dried embedded, I would have a place to hang the curtains I had made for the ten-by-twelve-inch entrance. I spent hours in the garden playing with my dollhouse, close to my uncle's woodworking shop.

This garden at Palazzo Santoro was where I developed a friendship with Maria, the housekeeper's daughter. The two of us spent time in the kitchen with her father, the chef, and then played through the house looking for her mother who was always busy cleaning. We eventually ended up in the attic, which was filled with dusty furniture. I loved playing in the attic.

Everything was so old in the house, including Signore Santoro, and because of his age and aloofness the townspeople sometimes gossiped about him.

He and his sister eventually both died, and the palazzo was inherited by the robust children of the chef and housekeeper.

Ciccillo (Francesco), and Mimi (Domenico)

MANY CHANGES

I Craved a Father

I knew that my Papa was in America. I wished that he were there for me in Santa Nicola. I didn't suffer from lack of attention; all my aunts and uncles were very attentive to me, without being demonstrative, but they weren't my Papa Giulio. With all the love that I was shown, it wasn't a hugging and touching kind of family, but I knew that I was loved and cared for.

I was lucky enough to be able to visit anyone at any time and always be welcomed in. If I showed up at the palazzo during the day and started to play with all my little friends in the walkway, Nonna Marzia walked out to greet me. She would comment about the noise and say lovingly, "Maria is here!" The walkway was only noisy when I arrived because my friends always ran out to play and sing with me in the courtyard.

Papa Giulio once sent home two pairs of shoes from America for Mamma, but they were size three so they only fit me. The shoes had very pointy toes, which everyone hated except me. I loved the idea that my Papa had sent something; I looked for anything that connected me to him.

Enclosed with the shoes was a letter written in Italian, with a sentence in the English language that ended, "and that's all!" Not knowing what the English words meant, Mamma continued to look for an additional package that never arrived.

A complete translation of the sentence revealed that Papa wrote, "I'm sending these shoes, and that's all!"

Mamma didn't find out until many years later what "and that's all!" meant.

One time my girlfriend's papa returned from America and took me along with her to the merry-go-round. I didn't like the idea of this man paying for my ride; I wished that it were my papa returning and being sporty enough to do this for my friend and me. It would have meant so much to me. I was jealous, but rationalized by thinking that maybe someday my Papa would do the same thing and I could pay my friend back.

The Cazzilli Family

Glorinda was another friend of mine. She was the older of two sisters in a family with seven brothers. This was a very well-to-do family, very respected by all the townspeople. Mamma was very close to them; they were her best customers and friends.

Their mother was quite busy with all her children and also very kind and generous to me. One more child added to the large group that she already had meant nothing to her; she always welcomed me.

Their father worked for the railroad. That was considered a very good job to have. Their uncle was the old blind priest in town. The family's oldest son was extremely talented. He made clothing for our dolls, duplicating all the styles we found in the fashion magazines. Not only did he make the dresses with handkerchief-length skirts, long in the back and short in the front, but also made the hats in style coordinated with the dresses. He created and stitched by hand all different types of fashions in styles from the 1920s to 1930s. The two sisters had the best-dressed dolls to play with.

The second-oldest son once made a shoebox stove for us. It had holes in the top and we actually cooked on it with a candle set underneath our doll pots and utensils. We took some oil and meat from the kitchen and made steak pizziola. We were so proud of ourselves for doing our own cooking that we even ate what we made.

Whenever we played in their house, we set up chairs in one of the empty wardrobes upstairs in the bedrooms and played make-believe train. One of the brothers imitated his papa and played conductor, while the rest of us, passengers, used little pieces of paper as tickets.

One time, Glorinda stole a cigarette from her oldest brother and we three girls went to hide in the bathroom to try it. She lit it with a match, coughed and gave it to me. I took my first and last puff of a cigarette that day. So did they. That cured us for the rest of our lives.

I went home sick, but didn't tell Mamma why I was sick.

The Sicilians

Soon after the cigarette episode, a handsome couple from Sicily came to the Maiello house to rent. The husband was in the army and was stationed in the area for at least a year. They were a lovely couple and had with them their two-year-old son, who was blond, blue-eyed and very precocious. I commented that he was always in the way when we had work to do! I was making beds with Zia Miluccia.

After a few months, this child became very sick and died. His parents prepared for the funeral; the wake was to be held in their apartment in the palazzo, as was customary for the times.

When I went upstairs to attend the wake with my family, we heard the mamma singing about the life of her dead son and how much she and her husband loved him. When she stopped singing, the papa picked up the song where she left off. In their bereavement they continued this singing. Our family thought this was very strange, but not knowing what Sicilians were like just took it as their custom. This was the first time that we had met Sicilians, and we couldn't understand their dialect or this very strange custom.

The couple sang until they buried their son.

A year later, the Sicilian couple was still renting from the Maiellos and within that time they had another baby. Everyone in the palazzo was pleased and very happy for them.

Courtyards

The center of life in each home was the courtyard. People were always around, especially at the palazzo courtyard, with the relatives, their spouses, children and tenants. Everyone worked together—preparing food, cleaning, and doing laundry —while the children played in our courtyard. The farm workers came to our courtyard early in the morning to start their day and again in the afternoon with their return from the fields. Their children came from school in the afternoon to join their parents. Zia Margarita served them all dinner in the courtyard.

In the courtyard, Mamma kept some chickens in a pen. One year she even kept a pig in that pen. She was charmed with the country life, having been born in the City of Caserta.

Life is music in Italy, and everyone really sang in the Province of

Napoli. They sang while they worked, they sang as they played. Whenever Mamma sewed on the sewing machine, in the family kitchen off the courtyard, she sang very loud over the noise of the machine! The townspeople even spread gossip by making up songs.

Every Neapolitan thought they had a voice, whether they did or not. Occasionally, when you strolled through town, you could hear people singing in the streets, sometimes in groups. There was Latin music in church and singing in school, but mostly singing was done in the courtyards. Sometimes a mandolin or guitar was played to accompany the singer. As we worked we listened to beautiful music coming from the courtyards.

When I learned the song, "*Funiculi, Funicula*" from my friends in Caiazzo, I couldn't stop singing it; I loved it so much. If I played with friends in the courtyard, and they heard me sing, they just joined in. If a passing adult heard us they also joined in. When we ran out of popular songs, we sang traditional songs.

The dance called the *tarantella* was done on occasion, but only in the courtyards behind the homes in our town, never in the streets. I watched the dancers performing, as they played their castanets, but I never danced; I was too reserved, too shy.

Courtyards were also used for the circuses when they came to town once a year. The circus was really a group of roving *zingari*, who arrived in fancy, colorful wagons, rented one of the bigger courtyards in town, and performed for a nominal fee. It was exciting to see them arrive; they drew everyone to them like magnets. The circus was not to be missed, as they had many acts, including a high-wire act with a trapeze artist.

One year the trapeze artist, the *zingara* who was the daughter of the circus owner and her papa got hurt when a live electrical wire crossed her high wire. It was a bad accident and I felt terrible about it. The poor people were really hurt badly.

This accident didn't stop the three of us from creating our own circus act every year after the circus left town. We strung up a high wire with pipes, wood, a bar and ropes in the courtyard of Zio Rocco's bakery. Ciccillo hung by his knees upside-down from the wire, and did a strong-arm act with Mimi and me hanging from his arms.

Then, all by himself as a special finale, Ciccillo hung upside-down by his toes and thoroughly entertained our audience, Zio Rocco's children, who had paid us a penny each for the show we put on in their courtyard.

Bacchus

My brother Mimi was such a beautiful child, with rosy cheeks, a strong, healthy look and his beautiful blond, blue-eyed coloring. He resembled the statue of the god of wine, Bacchus. The palazzo had this statue on the roof because Nonno Maiello had dealt in wines. The statue depicted Bacchus sitting on a barrel. The family called Mimi "Bacchus on the barrel."

Mimi hated it! He got so angry every time someone even mentioned it, and he chased anyone who tried to tease him with that name.

One day, Mimi was missing. We searched and searched for him all day long. We thought he was kidnapped or lost in the dangerous mountains behind the town. We just couldn't find him. Mamma was frantic. Because we spent the whole day looking for him without finding him, we all thought that he was abducted.

He was finally found at 9:00 p.m., sleeping on the flour sacks under Zio Rocco's bakery counter. Mamma was so relieved she didn't know whether to hug him or hit him.

Mimi would fall asleep wherever you put him; he had a clear head.

Adam's Rib, Destiny and Mal Occhio

From the time I was very young, I knew that Mamma had a scar from an operation. I could see it when she was washing herself. When I asked her about it, she reminded me of the story that Papa Sebastiano and Mamma Raffaela often told. She was five years old with a tumor under her arm. She described in detail the operation she had, and reminded me of the vows her parents made to the saints in heaven so that she would live. She claimed that was the reason she had such a hard life.

Mamma said that she didn't believe in vows. She believed that things should be left alone, in God's hands. Then she said that she could work hard like a man because, like Adam, she only had eleven ribs. Wasn't that a beautiful way to put it?

Mamma also believed in destiny. Like other people in town, she just accepted her lot in life. They all resigned themselves to whatever God had fated for them. Whenever anything bad happened, Mamma commented that it was her "*Destino Mio.*" She did this her whole life.

And as strong as her belief in God was, she also believed that if you got a bad headache, then someone was "overlooking you." *Mal Occhio* was the evil eye. If someone came to her for help because they had a headache, she began to pray very hard and get a soup dish out and add water to it. She sprinkled the water in the dish with olive oil as she prayed. If the oil settled into circles on the water and looked like eyes staring back at you, someone was wishing you *mal occhio*. If the oil dispersed in the water, then it was something else.

I never believed in it, so I wouldn't let Mamma do it for me when I had a headache.

Mamma always said that I didn't believe in everything she did.

Fifi Dorset

When I was seven years old, I was browsing through a French fashion magazine and saw a picture of Fifi Dorset. I was very impressed. I admired the style of her outfit and her haircut. Mamma, who was too busy in her store to do any sewing, sent me to the dressmaker in town, across the street from the grocery store, to have two dresses made. As I was leaving for my appointment with the dressmaker, Mamma gave me explicit instructions to have the dresses made with high necklines and at least three-quarter sleeves. "To show your elbow is the equivalent of showing your ass," she warned.

When I arrived at the dressmaker, I ignored Mamma's orders and instructed the woman to make both dresses with no sleeves, low circular necklines, short hemlines and a sash that had a bow on the side. When I returned home I didn't say anything to Mamma.

Weeks later the finished dresses arrived, and Mamma was shocked that I showed such independence and disregard for her orders. She was forced to pay the dressmaker for all her work on the improperly ordered dresses. And I got just what I wanted.

After the dress episode, I went to the barbershop to see Silvio, the young, handsome redheaded barber. No ladies' hairdresser for me! I told him to cut my hair very short in the back, like a boy's, and dip the sides forward to my cheeks and cut bangs across my forehead.

When I and returned home, the Veccia family was shocked. Mamma Raffaela said, "*Masculoni*!" What did you do? You look like a boy!

I responded with, "If the French can do it, so can I."

The Maiello aunts and uncles were charmed, and laughed about it when they saw me with my new haircut. They turned around, snickering and holding their mouths so I wouldn't see them.

But I did see them and I was proud of myself.

Mamma laughed. She knew that I had done it again. But with my new dresses and haircut, I finally got the look of Fifi Dorset that I had so admired in French fashion magazines.

Big Bows!

Every time I dressed up, Mamma pressed my pretty dresses and put a large bow in my hair. The bows were made of satin or silk and were tied onto my hair. I hated the bows, and no matter how much I fussed Mamma continued to do it.

The other little girls in town marveled at the large bows, and having parents who were not able to afford satin or silk, asked if they could touch the fabric. I hated the attention those bows got. I chased the girls away from me whenever they asked to touch them.

Quite often, Mamma took the three of us to the photographer in Caserta to have our pictures taken. The photographer's name was Galena, and he was a deaf mute. He was very high-strung and made us nervous with his actions, but he was an excellent photographer. Mamma took the finished pictures and sent them to Papa in America to show him how we were growing up.

There was only one time that I got away without wearing a bow in my hair for a picture. Mimi and I made our first Holy Communion together and I had to wear a veil for the ceremony. Good! No bows this time! But I didn't get away with very much that day. Mamma insisted that I wear fake curls pinned in front of my ears to hang on either side of the communion veil.

I often wondered what was worse; I looked so angry in that particular picture.

First Holy Communion
Mimi (Domenico) and Maria, with Ciccillo (Francesco)

My First Tragedy

Papa Sebastiano's Death

He had predicted the day and hour of his death. He died at the age of fifty-five from double pneumonia, and had recited his own last rites along with the priest.

I was only seven years old. I knew he was ill, and when I went up to the bedroom, he had just died. Mamma Raffaela said to me, "Maria, we have lost Papa."

I felt so lost. The only man I knew to have been a papa to me was gone. I loved and respected him so much. I couldn't cry because I saw my grandmother wasn't crying, but my heart was broken that he was gone.

I stood, dry-eyed, at the foot of the bed next to Mamma Raffaela, watching with her as Zia Filomena began to dress him in his best suit. Mamma had already left the room before I entered, probably to get Zio Rocco at the bread store.

The wake was held in their home, as was the custom. The relatives from Caserta, along with friends and neighbors, came to the house to pay their respects. Because he was so well known, everyone in town was in mourning with us, and in respect of Papa Sebastiano's death all the homes had their front doors half-closed.

I never entered Papa Sebastiano's bedroom again. I walked up the stairs, looked down the verandah to his door, but could never bring myself to enter.

Soon after the funeral, Mamma Raffaela must have felt just as I did because she left the bedroom that she shared with him and took another one in the same house, right over the grocery store.

Many weeks after the funeral, as I stood on the verandah near the stone railing just outside his old bedroom door, I concentrated on my memories of him. I didn't want to ever forget him and the love he showed me. I missed him terribly, and did this quite often, reliving everything.

I spent so much time on that verandah that I noticed a loose stone in the railing. When I moved it, because I thought it might hurt someone, I was very surprised to see bugs and worms under it, just like

Papa Sebastiano said in his favorite story about death. He was right there was no one here feeding these worms and yet they were big and healthy.

I gently put the stone back so as not to disturb the worms. Death had come for Papa Sebastiano; we would manage somehow because God was watching over us.

Mamma Raffaela's bedroom over the grocery store faced Mt. Vesuvius. I often stayed overnight with her after Papa Sebastiano died. In the grocery store there was an enclosed wooden staircase right near the counter. Most of the stairs in town were made of stone, but not this one. It took you up to the second floor bedrooms. You walked up the stairs and turned to the open balcony and then left to her bedroom.

This wooden staircase creaked when you walked on it, and reminded us all of Mamma's story about the Golden Boot. We visualized the mamma attempting to climb the stairs with only one leg: "THUMP! I made the first step..."

My Second Tragedy

Mamma and I spent a lot of time with Papa's three sisters, Zia Ninella, Zia Margarita and Zia Miluccia. Just being in their company was such a delight; it made life more pleasurable. As we worked together, sewing or cooking, we also laughed quite a lot together.

Zia Ninella was my beloved aunt who gave me a steak each day from my uncle's butcher shop. She had been admiring some beautiful flowers one day and said, "They are so beautiful that they make you want to die in order to get them."

It became a prophecy. She died from blood poisoning. She had a pimple that was lanced by a young, new doctor in town and died three days after the doctor's visit. Although the family should have blamed the doctor, they didn't. Every one was devastated.

During those three tragic days, Zia Angela Maria came from Caserta. She went to Zia Ninella's bedside and said, "I hurt too much to cry dear sister, I will cry for you when I feel better." She was so distraught that she had to be put to bed.

I couldn't go into Zia Ninella's bedroom as she lay dying. The memory of Papa Sebastiano's death was still too fresh.

Then, when it was close to the end, I went in to see her. I watched as she glanced up and chased away what she was seeing in her delirium. Then I saw her welcoming good visions and heard her say, "You can't have my children, only me."

Knowing that the end was near, the whole family was in her room when she died. In my grief, my chest hurt so much that it felt like a big, solid rock. Again I couldn't cry even though I was heartbroken.

Little Pierino and Sophia were left without their mother. Pierino was always my favorite, and Zia Margarita, in tears, told me, "You had better love both of them equally now."

Zia Ninella had died at the age of thirty, and four months pregnant. We hurt for her, her little children, and the child lost.

The funeral was held and many flowers were delivered to the house; she got her wish. The largest floral display was sent from Zia Ninella's first love, the paralyzed man. Her husband, Zio Totonno, said that even though his wife was dead, he was still jealous.

I had lost a loving aunt and it still hurts after so many years.

With great love and very much compassion, twenty-two-year-old Zia Margarita, took over, and raised her dead sister's children, Sophia and Pierino.

Zia Margarita was a great beauty, but because she was so thin she was lovingly called a "dry anchovy." Totonno the butcher eventually got lonely. He wanted to marry Zia Margarita's younger sister Zia Miluccia. Mamma felt that Zia Miluccia was too young for Totonno and stopped him from pursuing her. She thought that Zia Margarita was a better choice for him. He remained alone for many years.

Much later in life, Totonno Madonna married Zia Margarita. She was still a beauty and had lovingly raised his children. They went on to produce three more children together.

Zia Miluccia eventually married Paolo Ganzerli, and had one child.

Brazilian Angela Maria

The palazzo was very solemn and quiet in the days after Zia Ninella's death. People went on about their business and worked, but the laughter was gone from our lives; it was just too much of a tragedy.

A Brazilian cousin, another Angela Maria, came to visit, and treated me to a trip to Napoli for a few days. It was a welcome distraction. She had loads of money and was childless. She was a businesswoman who dealt in wedding gowns and had property in Rio de Janeiro, where she raised horses.

From Santa Nicola we took a train that had very plush compartments and velvet seats. When we arrived in Napoli, we went into a hotel overlooking the bay. After we were signed in at the desk, we rode the fancy elevators up to our room, and once we got settled, Angela Maria took me shopping.

We traveled from store to store, with Angela Maria shopping and filling a cedar chest for me with shoes, clothes and a china doll. She bought me beautiful silk dresses and then took me to a shoe store.

The clerk in the shoe store tried a pair of black patent leather shoes on me that I thought were the most beautiful things that I had ever seen. They were too small for me and they hurt my feet, but I was afraid to say something because I thought that they wouldn't have them in a larger size. The result was that I couldn't wear them once I got home because they hurt so much.

When we returned to Santa Nicola, Angela Maria asked Mamma if she could adopt me. She said that if she adopted me we would live quite well in Brazil and I would grow up to inherit her wealth.

Mamma sent a telegram to Papa in America that asked, "What is best for Maria?"

Papa sent a telegram back that stated, "Poor we are, poor we are going to stay!"

Angela Maria returned to Rio de Janeiro alone.

Ciccillo and Mimi

My brother Ciccillo was very talented. He had a beautiful singing voice and quickly learned songs he heard at weddings. He loved to sing the song called "*Cartolina e Napoli*," which was about a man who had gone away and yearned for his Napoli. He also mimicked the comedians and brought home their jokes and stories to perform for the family.

My brother Mimi was always the peacemaker and lover. Once when he was out with his girlfriend, *Cipolla*, in a tent, I was forced to interrupt his lovemaking.

I was sent by Mamma to get him home, "at once!" And when Mamma said it that way, we jumped.

Mimi told me, "You ruined it for me."

I was glad that I did.

I didn't know what was going on in the tent. I was too young to know what sex was; I just felt that it must be something bad. So I went home satisfied that I stopped something bad from happening.

Mimi was quick to forgive me. In 1928 the movie house in Caserta was showing a Charlie Chaplin movie, and he and Ciccillo decided to take me to see it.

We were all to get dressed in our finest clothes, which meant that I had to wear the baby fox wrap from Zio Pasquale that I hated. It had a full baby fox body with the head, eyes, tail and feet, and would clip together around my neck. I thought it was horrible.

Before leaving we went to show our grandmothers how we looked. Upon exiting the courtyard we heard a neighbor in the street exclaiming over us, "Just look at what their father is missing!" Ciccillo, with his dark hair, white skin and hazel eyes, Mimi, blue-eyed and platinum-haired, and me with my big green eyes and that baby fox wrap.

We started our walk to Caserta with my brothers holding me, one on each side. As we walked I tried to squirm out of the fox wrap. They held my arms so I couldn't.

We arrived at the movie house and watched the Charlie Chaplin film, which we all thoroughly enjoyed. Happy and exhausted after the movie, we walked back to Santa Nicola.

But how I hated that baby fox wrap.

Papa Giulio Sent 500 Lire

I was sitting on the stone bench by the fireplace in Nonna Marzia's family kitchen, and I really didn't feel very well. I ended up in bed and the doctor was called in. I was very ill; he diagnosed pneumonia and pleurisy. They expected me to die.

Papa was wired in America that if he wanted to see me alive he had better come right away. Mamma prayed to the Madonna of Pompeii and vowed to take me to the church in Pompeii if I lived. Papa stayed in America and sent 500 lire instead.

I remembered Mamma telling me that she didn't believe in vows. She told me that her life was hard because her parents prayed so hard for her when she was five years old and being operated on. Then, when

I was sick and given up for dead, she did the same thing with her prayers for me so that I might live.

Mamma created a necklace of peeled cloves of garlic strung on a long cord for me to wear. I hated it, but was too ill to complain very much. She and Mamma Raffaela took turns sitting and caring for me during my illness.

One night Mamma Raffaela fell asleep while she sat by my bed knitting a sock. When she woke up, the sock was finished; she had completed it in her sleep!

After many days I awoke one morning with blood gushing from my mouth and nose. I was choking as they put a basin to my face to catch the blood. Mamma called in the doctor and Zio Rocco. When the doctor came he said that I would start to feel better, the choking episode having cleared my lungs of the sickness.

When I finally recuperated, after many weeks, Mamma planned the trip to Pompeii. We left very early in the morning with a hired horse and buggy with driver. Mamma brought hardboiled eggs, bread, fruit and snacks for the long trip. We had eaten no breakfast because we were to receive communion in church.

I got motion sickness from the horse and buggy ride. When we arrived in Pompeii we first went to mass and said prayers of thanksgiving to the Madonna of Pompeii for my restored health. The Black Madonna, as she was called, was always depicted as black from the volcanic ash. Everyone took communion at mass except me, I was too sick. After mass, Mamma, Ciccillo, Mimi and I ate breakfast and I started to feel better.

We then walked to view the new Town of Pompeii, then old Pompeii. Old Pompeii was nothing but houses with destroyed ceilings, just walls remaining in barren land with no trees and no shade. As the day progressed, it became very hot outside.

Escaping from the heat, we went into the museum that housed plaster casts made from the hollowed-out remains of the dead bodies. The guide explained how the casts were made.

I was very intrigued with the casts that showed bodies with details so minute that you could even see fingernails and faces showing their last scream.

After a very long day, the horse and buggy took us home to Santa Nicola.

My Third Tragedy

Upstairs from Mamma Raffaela, on the third floor, lived Matteo and his family. Matteo was about eight years old, my age at the time. His mother's name was Gennerina.

Mamma and Gennerina were very close to each other. When we visited her and her family, Matteo always told everyone that he was getting a ladder and stealing me off to marry me! The adults just laughed when he said this. I was totally indifferent to him.

Gennerina's husband was a horrible man who beat all his children. He had a wooden leg because he had fallen from a tree and lost his real one. He used the wooden leg to kick his children against the stone walls.

The man was a shoemaker who only repaired shoes in his shop. His shop was located right next to Mamma's grocery store.

My third tragedy was watching their two-year-old child die. Gennerina's husband wouldn't let his wife give the little girl water as she lay close to dying. The little one was such a beautiful child. She had very large, luminous eyes, and in her fever and dying they haunted me.

The papa said to Gennerina, Don't give her any water, she's dead anyway."

Gennerina just cried until her baby died.

For the funeral, Gennerina dressed her little dead daughter in a white dress and veil, just like we girls wore for our first Holy Communion. It was so sad to see.

I just got my satisfaction by hating that man.

Spring Rainy Season

So the crops were planted again, and another year of harvest would come. I still ran, whenever I could get away, to escape to my fields of poppies to see them in bloom. And I wanted wooden shoes. I always wanted wooden shoes. Some of my friends owned them, and no matter how many times I asked Mamma, she always told me, "No."

I loved the click, click sound they made on the pavement. Mamma said I couldn't have them because only farmers wore them and we weren't farmers. The farmers didn't have the means for leather shoes; whatever monies came in from produce was not enough for the nicer things in life.

Next to Mamma's grocery store was Gennerina's husband's store. He was the shoemaker in town who only repaired shoes.

The other shoemaker in town was located further down the Via Santa Croce, past the post office. We went to him often. He would take our measurements and make leather shoes for us by hand.

He and his wife were a lovely couple who were crazy about the three of us. They were very sad because they had suffered the tragedy of losing three stillborn babies. They made such a fuss over us whenever we went to visit. When they eventually had two daughters we were very happy for them.

One of my greatest pleasures in life was to splash in puddles during the April rainy season. I'd go walking in the rain and unintentionally ruin the shoes he made. I probably would have done better with the wooden shoes that I wanted so badly; at least they would have been more difficult to destroy.

Donna Elena

It seemed that we were always in church, which was right across the street facing the grocery store. Mamma heard the mass in progress from the store, and, while she worked, recited it in Latin as it progressed.

Every night I went to mass with Mamma Raffaela, even when we visited her sister, Zia Maria Antonia, in Caiazzo. The church in Santa Nicola had a very fat, old blind priest who was retired and couldn't say mass anymore. He was the uncle of my friend Glorinda. He had a four-room apartment in the Cazzilli house, down the Via Santa Croce before it turned to become the Via San Marco. You could see the house from the side of the church. He had a housekeeper named Donna Elena to cook for him and take care of his apartment.

One day I went with Glorinda to the priest's place to visit. She walked me through his rooms and I asked my friend why the apartment had only one bed?

My friend replied, "Because Donna Elena sleeps with my Uncle."

After that visit, Donna Elena wanted help cutting out a dress pattern and she asked Mamma for assistance. When Mamma started to leave to help her, she told me where she was going. I started to cry. I put up such a tremendous fuss and Mamma didn't know why.

I didn't explain to her until years later that I got upset that day because I didn't want her to associate with a "fallen woman." I thought that associating with her would contaminate Mamma.

Bad Dreams

I sometimes suffered nightmares. It was always the same recurrent theme: A man was coming down the chimney. I dreamt that love was walking toward me and I was receptive to the love. It was to envelop me. When he got closer, I saw so much malice in his face that terror and fear struck at my heart and I woke up shaking!

I'd run out to the sunlit step in the doorway and sit all alone to compose myself. I sat in the sun until my heart stopped pounding.

I was always alone. Mamma was already in the store and my brothers were up, dressed and gone. I never told Mamma or anyone about my nightmares. Not even running to my aunts for comfort, I was embarrassed to show weakness.

I was also very quiet and deep thinking; no one ever knew what I thought about. For a small child, I had a deep sense of understanding, sympathy and compassion, very great compassion.

Even as a young girl I felt so bad for my aunt, Zia Addolorada, understanding how she missed her husband just as I missed my papa.

The Maiello family spoke so often about their dead Papa Francesco that we children felt as if we knew our grandfather. With his death, I was told that my Papa was never the same, and I could feel his pain at losing his papa, even though I lacked my papa's presence and really didn't know him.

I never got caught visiting my cousin Marzia, Zio Filippo's daughter. She used to tell me, "We are not just friends, we are cousins." I acted like I didn't understand her when she said it.

If Nonna Marzia ever found out that I was visiting her, I think she would have killed me for going against her orders. As good-hearted and generous as the Maiellos are, WATCH OUT when they are provoked to anger. But my pity always stepped in, not wanting to hurt my cousin.

We all learn what we live. I lived with love and compassion from Mamma and Papa Veccia and my aunts and uncles. I saw such strength and determination in Nonna Marzia that I hesitated to show any weakness. I was shown decency and respect by the townspeople. I grew respectful and compassionate from it.

But the recurrent bad dreams? Things were changing in our little town as in all of Italy.

A DECISION IS MADE

The Fascist Movement, 1928

I knew that we had to have the *fascia* book in our home and that all our names had to be listed in it. My brother Ciccillo hated it and hated Mussolini. My brother Mimi never gave an opinion.

The youth of the country were generally taken up in the movement, with the music, the uniforms, the marching. Everyone was jumping into the excitement, but really just falling into a pit.

I was excited about my uniform. I loved my pleated skirt, over-blouse and little matching hat. I wore the uniform when there was to be a parade.

But I grew to know that my elders were living in fear, and I thought that forcing people was wrong. The militia forced everyone to join. We were forced to have the *fascia* book and follow the rules in it. The militiamen showed up in the stores and looked for something to make trouble about. Gossip was spread that if you didn't comply with the militia orders they forced you to drink castor oil.

The militia went to Zia Carmela's *gelati* store in Caserta, and she became so upset and frightened that she died. What a terrible time it was.

They even came to Mamma's grocery store to complain about the bread Mamma sold from Zio Rocco's bakery. The militia said that it wasn't baked long enough. That did it for Mamma. She wasn't going to let her sons get involved in the coming war.

Mamma made the difficult decision to go to America because of the power of dictatorship warning her that there were only black days ahead. She wrote to Papa with news of the militia visit and Zia Carmela's death. When she wrote that letter she gave him an ultimatum: "It's

Papa Giulio in America

now you had better get busy!" She really didn't want to leave Mamma Raffaela, her grocery store and her life as it existed, but feared she had to leave to save her sons.

We children knew what was going on. We were very quiet about it, not showing any emotions at all, never asking any questions. Mamma's biggest concern was money: she planned to move back in with Mamma Raffaela so she could rent out our apartment in the palazzo and collect rent from it.

In the Meantime in America

Papa was working as a foreman in construction and giving jobs to men who arrived from our hometown. He had compassion for the poor and unemployed, and was very generous to them. He knew that we were being well taken care of by Mamma and the two families.

He himself was enjoying wine, women and song and spending almost every penny he made, which was $115 a week until he was hurt in a construction accident.

Papa fell five stories when a crane knocked him off a scaffold. He said good-bye to himself in midair and landed in a wheelbarrow. Instead of dying, he got up and walked away from the accident with only a broken wrist. He was home on compensation waiting for his case to be heard.

When he received the letter from Mamma stating that she was planning to come to America, he knew that she meant business. He also knew that she would cut ties with him forever if he rejected her demand.

He understood that she was worried about the militia bothering her again. He knew her concerns about the *Fascisti* and Mussolini, and her fear that Ciccillo might be conscripted into service. From the newspapers, which he always read, he, too, saw how things were changing and realized why she wanted no part of it.

He wrote back to tell her to come to America. Then he went to apply for his citizenship papers, which, in that year only, also started the naturalization process for us while we were still living in Italy.

Vesuvius, 1929

Mamma Raffaela's apartment had a balcony that faced Mt. Vesuvius. She had such a beautiful view from this balcony, which was right over the grocery store. Once Papa Sebastiano was gone, she took this room, and I loved staying overnight with her so she wouldn't be lonely.

One night we both slept through an eruption of Mt. Vesuvius. There was also an earthquake that night, and Mamma rushed from the palazzo to see if we were all right. Our house was fine and we had both slept through the rumblings. The only catastrophe we had was the destruction of my dollhouse that my brothers had made for me. It cracked right down the middle, but the two halves stayed together.

There was great devastation in neighboring towns, with some houses having their second stories collapsing onto the first-floor rooms. The relief workers brought people from those towns to Santa Nicola for temporary shelter. There were no casualties but many people were hurt and bandaged.

When a man in one devastated house awoke and reached out to the oil lamp by the side of his bed, he grabbed a chicken instead of his lamp. His bed had fallen into the chicken roost on the first floor!

This eruption and earthquake made me a fanatic: again, the Maiello cleanliness disease. When I watched from the balcony and saw some people with bandaged heads, arms, and legs, and saw the relief trucks with doctors and nurses helping people. The relief trucks had pictures of women being pulled out of the rubble and rocks. I decided that every night I had to wash every part of my body extra clean, because if they ever had to pull me out of an earthquake like the women in those pictures, I just had to smell really clean. I never thought about just how much dirt was going to fall on me. This part of my life never left me.

Soon after the eruption, Mamma found a tenant for our palazzo apartment. The Sicilian couple took it and we all moved in with Mamma Raffaela. Zio Nicola was still a young bachelor. Mamma set out to find her brother a wife. She found Nannina, an orphan brought up by a lovely couple. Mamma figured that being an orphan Nannina would be more understanding of the position the family was in without Papa Sebastiano.

The match and wedding took place. Mamma turned over the grocery store to her brother, Nicola, along with all the ledgers and monies. She kept nothing for herself. She felt that she and her children were well fed and clothed and that was her payment for all the years of running the store.

Mamma Raffaela begged her to hold back some money for herself to help with the passage to America. Mamma took none.

PASSPORT

Our passport

November 1929: Passport

The harvest season was over in the palazzo. The tomato canning was done. The men had killed the yearly pig to make into sausages and *prosciutto.* Zia Margarita was caring for Sofia and Pierino, and we took our walk to the cemetery for All Saints' Day and All Souls' Day. We had too many fresh memories of painful times: Zia Ninella and Papa Sebastiano's deaths. And now yet another change; we were going to America.

Mamma received a reply from Papa in America. Once Mamma learned from Papa that he had gone to apply for his citizenship papers she started our end of the process.

The four of us took a horse and buggy trip to the American Consulate in Napoli for our passports. When we arrived, the consulate was locked tight, closed for the American holiday, Thanksgiving. We planned on returning another day.

Instead of going straight home we went to visit Mamma's friend in the nearby Town of Pozzuoli. Not understanding anything about the American holiday, we told Mamma's friend what had happened at the consulate.

Mamma's friend explained, with her limited knowledge, the story of the American Thanksgiving holiday to us.

We listened to the story and responded, "Stupid Americans have a holiday for chickens!"

On our second trip to the American Consulate, we were all subjected to physical examinations. Everyone checked out fine except me. They found trouble with my eyesight and said that I had astigmatism. I was put under a doctor's care and given drops to use in my eyes. We were held back for three months while I was under the doctor's care.

You had to be perfect to go to America.

Embroidery Class

So life in our little town went on, with Zio Nicola running the grocery store and Mamma preparing for America, collecting rent from our apartment in the palazzo and another one she had purchased.

Ciccillo was in high school in Caserta, Mimi and I still attended school in Santa Nicola, and I continued my embroidery classes.

My embroidery teacher made linens for the bridal trousseau of the daughter of the Amatos, the mill people in the Town of Santa Maria. Nine years old, I was chosen by the teacher to do the art of precision pulling of threads that would create angels. Some of these stitches were called four hundred; some were called five hundred.

In four hundred embroidery you pulled three threads, leaving three horizontal and then three vertical. You created a pattern of little squares and then embroidered an angel on it. In five hundred embroidery you created the angel first and then filled in the squares. No easy task!

When the teacher heard we were planning to leave for America she got the bright idea that I should make a window panel for her two French windows that opened into the room. Each window was about one and a half yards tall.

She decided that I should make one panel and complete it before leaving for America. My friend worked on the other panel. This was all open cutwork, and I worked like a dog to finish it. This window panel was for my teacher to remember me after I went to America. She should have given me a gift for all that hard work, not to mention what it cost Mamma in groceries to pay for my lessons.

But, I felt sorry for my embroidery teacher, as she was an only daughter and an old maid. She was all of forty-something, so who would marry her, with an invalid mother who couldn't get out of bed?

My teacher had to take care of her mother every day. She washed her every morning and served her three meals a day in bed. When her mother had to use a bedpan (remember this was one large studio apartment) we girls in class wanted to run for cover. We needed fresh air, but couldn't make a face about the smell; just keep a stiff upper lip, as the British would say.

It's no wonder that every Saturday the teacher took one of the girls from the class with her to Caserta to buy thread. She left her mother alone only that one day a week.

When we arrived in Caserta, she left whichever girl she brought with her on a park bench and was gone for a couple of hours.

When we girls discussed it we suspected a secret lover, or the big house of ill repute that Caserta was noted for, among other things. It was completely government-run and inspected.

Who could blame this poor woman for her little weekly indiscretion?

A Bad Situation Made Worse

We spent our last holidays in Italy with Zio Rocco and his family, and Zia Carolina, who was still living next door with Zio Totonno and their children. *Buon Natale* was again somber without Papa Sebastiano with us.

When the Lenten season approached, the basin of water was again set up in the palazzo courtyard for us to look for Salome and Herodias riding on a beam of fire for all eternity. At *Buona Pasqua* we had our last picnic, with all the home-baked specialties, at the Palazzo Reale in Caserta.

My brothers and I didn't discuss our move to America and still didn't ask any questions, just followed orders and did what we had to do.

Evidently, the bride Mamma chose for Zio Nicola was not as she expected. Nannina complained to Nicola that she only married one man, not a mother, sister and three children!

Zio Nicola didn't want to talk to his sister about his wife's complaint. Mamma had been so good to him, setting him up in the store, but Naninna pushed him into it.

When Mamma heard of Naninna's complaint she went to her brother Rocco for help and Rocco in turn approached the relatives in Caserta.

There was a big meeting when the relatives arrived from Caserta. They came to discuss our situation and plead our case to Nannina. After their discussion, it was agreed that Mamma could stay on for a couple of months only.

Without work there was no income for Mamma, and we were going to lose the roof over our heads. At that point Mamma was shedding too many tears about her *destino*, and I was waiting for my eyes to get better (while still working on the window embroidery panel).

Nonna Marzia stepped in to tell us that we still had an entitled room at the palazzo. But our original room at the top of the stairs was rented out to the Sicilian couple along with another room Mamma had also purchased and was renting. So the four of us moved in with Nonna and spent the remainder of our time in Italy back at the palazzo.

One day just before we moved out of Mamma Raffaela's house, she visited Zio Rocco to see if he needed any help with the children, and then returned to the grocery store. She had made a package of 500 lire that she had saved and was going to give it to Mamma for the passage to America. This was considered a lot of money.

While she was outside the counter in the store, she slipped the package of money into her bra. During the course of the day she was unaware that the package had slipped out of her clothing. When she finally realized that the money was gone, she searched frantically all over the store. When she didn't find it she realized that someone had probably picked it up and walked off with it.

Mamma Raffaela was so upset; there were terrible, bitter tears between the lost money and the situation that Nannina caused.

Zio Nicola was very unhappy about being pushed by Nannina; his sister had worked all those years in the store and been so good to him.

And Mamma had finally resigned herself to the fact that we needed to make this temporary move.

Back to the Palazzo

So we were finally back to the ghost in the well and the wall of monk's fat and sleeping in Nonna Marzia's apartment.

Mamma decided to set up one of the first-floor storage rooms as a kitchen for us. Since she always worked she never learned how to cook. Once she turned the store over to her brother Nicola, she finally had time to practice and learn.

She cooked little meals and served them. Everyone commented that the food she prepared was delicious, but whatever she made always needed just a little more salt.

Quite often I went to sleep with Mamma Raffaela in her house. I missed her at night and knew she was lonely with the four of us gone to the palazzo.

Spring planting season came again, and then the spring rains, and the poppies in the fields bloomed even more beautifully that year. I still ran, whenever I could, to see them in all their glory.

And I still laughed with the farm workers when they teased each other, and helped serve them their evening meals with Zia Margarita, and Mamma cooking and baking rounds of bread. And Zia Miluccia and I still made beds together in the mornings.

We visited Zia Maria Antonia in Caiazzo, Zia Filomena in Paoliso, and relatives in Caserta. I still played and sang with my friends in the courtyard.

Papa wrote to Mamma and told her he got his citizenship papers. Mamma wrote to Papa's brother, Domenico, and his wife, Serafina, in Brazil, to tell them about us going to America. Her biggest concern was still money.

Life went on as usual in Santa Nicola, but the militia were everywhere and coming around more and more.

Dangerous Mountain

In Santa Nicola there is another alleyway in back of the houses, that goes to the foot of a mountain. It was very dangerous by day, and worse alone in the dark of night. The area was filled with big boulders, rocks and snakes, and was actually the quarry where the stone was cut to build the town's houses.

Only once or twice have I seen my brother Ciccillo act rebellious. God knows he had reason to be so. One night, he decided to run away from home. Where did he go? *Basso u Monde* at night?

When we realized he was gone we searched for him all day. Aunts and uncles from both sides of the family joined in to help look for him. Mamma was like a madwoman searching for him. First because he had a special place in her heart, and second, she feared losing him and was hurt that he did this to her because she had always done so much for us.

By the time we finally found him, Mamma was so upset that she cried as she beat him severely for scaring her. I never saw Mamma like this before. The family had to literally pull him away from her to protect him from her fury.

It's no wonder Ciccillo does not remember this episode.

Skulls and Bones

The church of Santa Nicola had what is called an *ossuario.* It was located in the cellar of the church and was used as the receptacle for the bones of all the deceased priests and nuns once their bodies had disintegrated in the crypts. After so many years in the crypts, the bones were disinterred and put in the cellar so the blessings of the masses would continue over them.

Mamma had developed a goiter. She didn't want to leave for America with it. She was told by some of the townspeople that if she wanted to get rid of it she had to go to the *ossuario* and urinate on the bones of the dead.

Mamma decided to sneak into the *ossuario.* She took her seventeen-year-old sister-in-law Zia Miluccia with her to sneak into the church and climb down into the *ossuario* through a trapdoor. They didn't want to get caught because they dreaded having to explain their reason for being there.

As they reached the trapdoor their fears grew with the realization of what they were doing. They climbed through the trapdoor and down the ladder, into the large cellar with bones and skulls stacked up and laying all over the room. Both of them were very afraid.

Mamma, wanting to leave this room as quickly as possible, soon found a spot and started to urinate on the bones, as she was instructed.

Zia Miluccia noticed one of the skulls seemed to be staring at her. She became mesmerized by this one particular skull and stared back at it. When she heard the sizzling noise her sister-in-law was making, she thought the skull was moving

Zia Miluccia said, "Vincenzella, hurry up. I think this one is coming alive. We are invading their privacy."

Mamma couldn't stop laughing. But, spooked and scared, they left that place very quickly.

This escapade of Mamma's did nothing to cure her goiter. She had to resort to visiting a doctor, who cleared it up with only one injection.

It never returned.

Last Trip to the Consulate

We took our third and final trip to the American Consulate in Napoli, where we were examined and given clearance. Our passports were issued finally on August 7, 1930, during the mid-summer harvest.

The Sicilian couple who rented our room had left the palazzo, the husband's tour of duty over, and returned to Sicily with their baby. We stayed with Nonna Marzia, and Mamma sold her bedroom set from our room to a new bride. She also sold her copper cook set and the glass-front cabinet it was displayed in, plus her china cabinet. She kept only the large trunk for us to move our clothing to America and to carry her linens, embroidered sheets and tablecloths.

After All Saints' Day and a final trip to the cemetery, our emigration visa was issued on November 28, 1930. A whole year had gone by.

On the morning we were to leave Italy we had to get up at 4:00 a.m. for our horse and buggy trip to the Port of Napoli. When we arose, Nonna Marzia met us in the family kitchen with a fresh pot of espresso, and all the Maiello relatives—aunts, uncles and cousins surprised us by getting up to say good-bye.

We sat in Nonna's kitchen for the last time having coffee and breakfast together. With words of encouragement for the journey to our new home, the relatives told us there were no werewolves in America. They explained that unlike the winding streets in Italy, the streets in America were straight and all "made the sign of the cross," so no more werewolves.

They sent us off in the dark, with love, laughter and bags of sweet lemons and a bottle of Fernet Branca for the voyage.

They had made our final months in Italy a lot of fun.

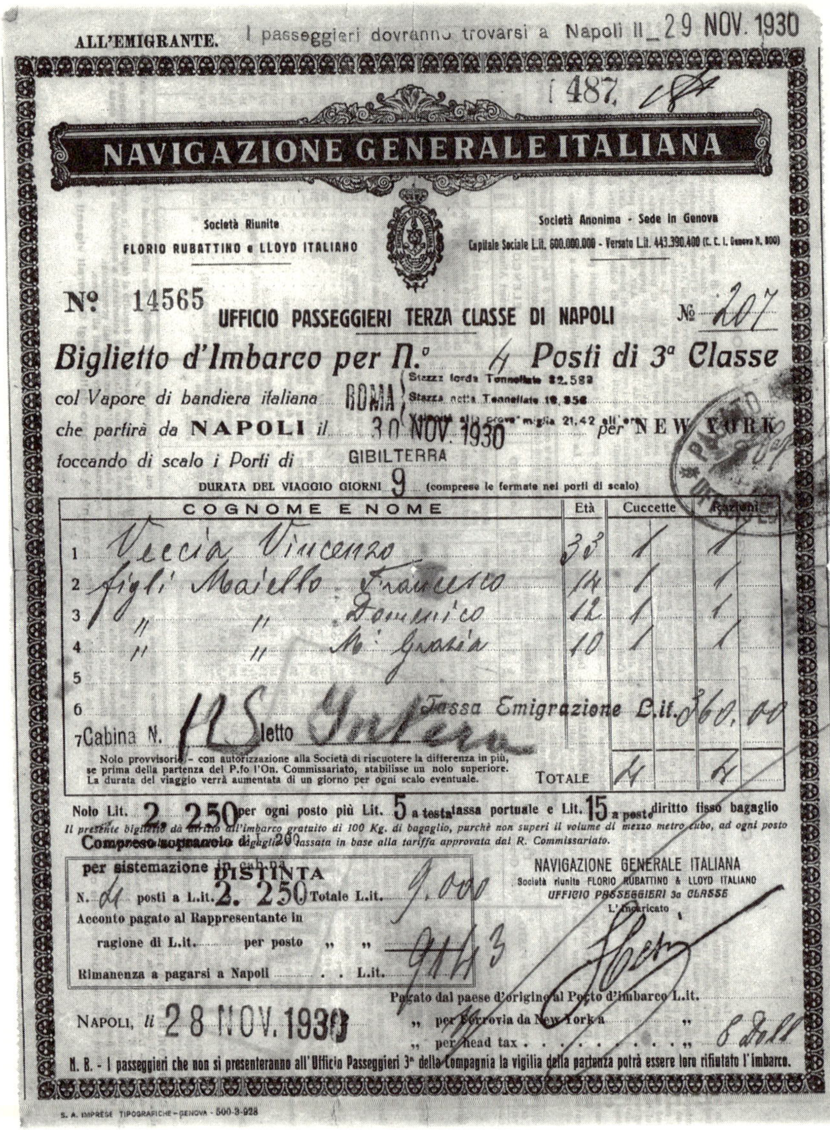

ALL'EMIGRANTE. I passeggieri dovranno trovarsi a Napoli il 29 NOV. 1930

487

NAVIGAZIONE GENERALE ITALIANA

Società Riunite FLORIO RUBATTINO e LLOYD ITALIANO

Società Anonima - Sede in Genova
Capitale Sociale L.it. 600.000.000 - Versato L.it. 443.390.400

Nº 14565 UFFICIO PASSEGGIERI TERZA CLASSE DI NAPOLI № 207

Biglietto d'Imbarco per N.° 4 Posti di 3ª Classe

col Vapore di bandiera italiana ROMA Stazza lorda Tonnellate 32.583 Stazza netta Tonnellate 19.356

che partirà da NAPOLI il 30 NOV. 1930 per NEW YORK

toccando di scalo i Porti di GIBILTERRA

DURATA DEL VIAGGIO GIORNI 9 (comprese le fermate nei porti di scalo)

	COGNOME E NOME	Età	Cuccette	Razioni
1	Veccia Vincenzo	35	1	1
2	figli Maiello Francesco	14	1	1
3	" " Domenico	12	1	1
4	" " M. Grazia	10	1	1
5				
6	Tassa Emigrazione L.it. 360,00			
7	Cabina N. letto			
	Nolo provvisorio - con autorizzazione alla Società di riscuotere la differenza in più, se prima della partenza del P.fo l'On. Commissariato, stabilisse un nolo superiore. La durata del viaggio verrà aumentata di un giorno per ogni scalo eventuale. TOTALE		4	4

Nolo Lit. 2.250 per ogni posto più Lit. 5 a testa tassa portuale e Lit. 15 a posto diritto fisso bagaglio

Il presente biglietto dà diritto all'imbarco gratuito di 100 Kg. di bagaglio, purchè non superi il volume di mezzo metro cubo, ad ogni posto ... bagaglio tassata in base alla tariffa approvata dal R. Commissariato.

Compreso soprannolo di L. 200 per sistemazione in cabina

DISTINTA

N. 4 posti a L.it. 2.250 Totale L.it. 9.000

Acconto pagato al Rappresentante in ragione di L.it. per posto " "

Rimanenza a pagarsi a Napoli L.it. 9443

NAVIGAZIONE GENERALE ITALIANA
Società riunite FLORIO RUBATTINO & LLOYD ITALIANO
UFFICIO PASSEGGIERI 3a CLASSE
L'Incaricato

Pagato dal paese d'origine al Porto d'imbarco L.it.
" per Ferrovia da New York a "
" per head tax . . . . " 8 Doll

NAPOLI, li 28 NOV. 1930

N. B. - I passeggieri che non si presenteranno all'Ufficio Passeggieri 3ª della Compagnia la vigilia della partenza potrà essere loro rifiutato l'imbarco.

S. A. IMPRESE TIPOGRAFICHE - GENOVA - 500-3-928

Emigration document

Leaving Italy

Zio Rocco, Mamma Raffaela and Zio Nicola took the four of us by horse and buggy, to the Port of Napoli. When we finally arrived, the porters took the large trunk with all our belongings that Mamma had brought with us for the voyage.

We all had to walk along the beach to get to the ship. We were separated from them when a large fence was closed, and we were forced to kiss good-bye through the bars.

Mamma Raffaela took a chain from around her neck and slipped a small 18K gold medallion off it. It was a number 13, which she explained to me was a special number because it signified St. Anthony's birthday, June 13th. She told me to keep it always as a remembrance of her. Her eyes filled up with tears and so did mine but we both kept our dignity. Again, as much as it hurt me to leave her and as sad as I was, I couldn't cry. Only Mamma was crying.

We left from the Port of Napoli on November 30, 1930, on the ship "Roma."

Zio Rocco and Zio Nicola took a little rowboat out into the bay and followed the ship in it. They were rowing and waving to us from the little rowboat until our ship left the harbor. Zio Rocco waved a final good-bye. Zio Nicola just kept his head down. He couldn't look up to wave good-bye.

Mamma was sitting, watching as we waved to them in the rowboat, and with tears streaming down her cheeks she completely broke down.

Voyage to America

We had a third-class room with two bunk beds. Mamma, Ciccillo and I were seasick during the entire eight-day voyage. All we could try to eat were the sweet lemons we had brought from home, to settle our stomachs. The first two days and last two days were a little better for us than the deep ocean, mid-Atlantic roughness.

During those four rotten middle days nothing we tried to eat stayed down. Mamma tried the Fernet; even that didn't work. We couldn't lift our heads off the bunk bed pillows, except to be sick. I just wanted to die.

Completely unaffected, my brother Mimi loved the ship and ran and played during the entire crossing.

At the beginning of the voyage, our family met a woman all dressed in black, with an eight-year-old daughter and a four-year-old son.

The two Mammas became friends on the ship. As we neared our destination, Mamma wondered to her new friend if they would ever meet again.

The woman in black replied, "Mountains to mountains don't meet, but people do. We will see each other again someday."

I was sad to leave Italy but I knew that my most important wish was coming true. I would finally have the papa that I craved so much. I knew with a great empty sadness that I would miss everyone; I missed them already, but I was glad to be getting away from the ghosts, witches and monk's fat. I wouldn't miss the threat of Vesuvius and my fear of it. No werewolves in America? Good; no more monsters!

But I was so seasick on that ship that I reached the point where I couldn't think or feel anything anymore and just wanted to be back on land again.

I didn't know that I would be going to real monsters in America. Not yet, anyway.

America

We arrived in New York harbor on December 8, 1930. We saw the Statue of Liberty from the ship and knew that she meant freedom. No *fascia* books were to be kept in America, except as a token of what we had left behind.

We had to go through Ellis Island immigration, and it took most of the day because of the great volume of people on the ship.

We were exhausted, waiting in a great big room, until Mamma said, "That's your papa," and we watched him as he walked up a very large staircase toward us. We were so happy to finally be introduced to our papa and instantly saw looks and mannerisms in him that reminded us of the uncles we had left behind in Italy. We felt familiar with him.

It was night by the time we took a taxi to the apartment that Papa had rented and furnished for us in Brooklyn, at 146 20th Street, between Third and Fourth Avenues.

Mamma's large trunk with all our belongings had broken the fender on the taxi! Papa had an argument with the cab driver over it.

Italy had been warm; New York in December was so cold. Ciccillo and Mimi were wearing short pants and we were freezing, but I was almost eleven years old and my secret prayer had finally been answered, at last I had a papa.

But, America was in the Great Depression, and Papa was unemployed and waiting for a hearing and a decision on his compensation case.

This voyage ended what I soon came to learn was the happiest time of my life, my innocent youth.

EPILOGUE

Epilogue

The relatives we left behind in Italy showed us, with their dignity and undemonstrative natures, a depth of love so strong and powerful and infinitely pure as to be noble and Godlike in its existence. We received tremendous love from them.

Yet, growing up surrounded by all this love, I never believed in the concept of destiny they all had. I just didn't believe it. I always felt that you made your own destiny, but always with the help of God. We make our own choices and He's there if and when we fall, ready with a helping hand. You just have to get up, shake the dust off and start again, with no tears, just a strong determination to go on. And that is just what I did. I had to.

By way of explanation, the Town of Santa Nicola La Strada was in the Province of Naples during the years we lived there. The area has subsequently alternated between being in the Province of Naples and the Province of Caserta.

The love story of my maternal grandparents, Sebastiano and Raffaela, always reminded me of the 1944 Robert Young, Dorothy McGuire movie called The Enchanted Cottage. The movie was about two people who fell so deeply in love that they believed they had undergone tremendous physical changes, when it was only their love for each other that made them perfect in each other's eyes.

Mamma received a letter in America many years after we left Italy. It told of the town priest, who had listened to a confession about the "lost money" picked up in the store that day after my grandmother Raffaela had accidentally dropped it.

The priest said the person who took it was giving him so much a month until it was paid in full. The priest brought the money across the street and handed it to my Uncle Nicola in the store. I said, at the time, "A lot of good it does Mamma now." But along with her I was happy to know that a wrong had been righted.

Uncle Rocco eventually became the mayor of the Town of Santa Nicola. He lived to a great old age, with his sons taking over and running the bakery. His daughter, Filomena, went on to become a teacher in Naples. He and Mamma kept their close relationship by mail throughout their years.

With such great sadness, Mamma never saw her mother Raffaela or brother Nicola again. This was always her biggest regret in life. Raffaela died in 1949 at the age of eighty-two, and my Uncle Nicola died from spinal meningitis in 1951, at the age of forty-one. His daughter, Raffaelina, corresponded with Mamma, and when Mamma went to Italy to visit in 1960, the rift that had been created by her mother Nannina when we left was mended with many tears by Naninna and her daughter. Raffaelina was very good to Mamma, and Mamma became very close to her and corresponded with her for the rest of her life.

On my grandmother Raffaela's sisters in Caiazzo, one of the two sons that went to Connecticut, the cousin named Poppolizzio, went on to become the mayor of New Haven.

Gennerina's husband, the shoemaker with the wooden leg, died of some mysterious illness. I truly believe that he was the only man I ever hated. May God forgive him for his cruelty to his children.

Mamma did indeed meet the woman again that she met on the ship. She not only met her but they became neighbors and friends when the woman and her family moved onto the same block that we were living on in a suburban village on Long Island. They watched their daughters and sons-in-law develop a close lifetime friendship, and also watched their grandchildren playing together. We all spent many happy times together.

In 1988 I was so happy to finally meet my aunt Serafina in Rio de Janeiro, Brazil. I remembered all the prayers we said as children for her and my uncle Domenico. When we met she was very old, still very beautiful, warm, loving and thoroughly charming. It was a wonderful moment for both of us. Her daughters, my four cousins, are just like her, beautiful, warm and loving. When I asked her about her famous portrait, the one painted by the starving artist in gratitude to my uncle for helping him, she told me she had given it to the maid. When I asked her why she did that, she explained, "Because I was painted with a flower in my hair and I never liked the portrait!"

My great aunt Maria Antonia is forever in my heart and prayers. I think today of how lucky I was to have people like her and Mamma in my early life. They were such great teachers. I used to absorb everything like a sponge from them.

Of my holy, loving, grandfather, Sebastiano, my sweet grandmother, Raffaela, my strong and talented grandmother, Marzia, I think God must have graced me from the moment of conception to bless me with having these kinds of saints around me.

And let's not forget my uncle, the wood carver Totonno, the kind of man that I hoped to marry one day. When I grew up that is exactly what I did. I found an Anthony who was tall, handsome, kind and entertaining, just like my uncle. And my husband's birthday was June 13th, St. Anthony's feast day!

Was it coincidence that my grandmother Raffaela gave me that medallion, or did she see the marriage for me in my future? Who knows? Neapolitans are like that.

My husband Tony even put up with my remnant of the Maiello cleanliness curse left over from the eruption of Vesuvius that day.

When we first married he would say, "You never come out of that bathroom. Even if I wanted to fool around a little, you take so long in there, the feeling is gone now!"

I'd laugh as I was washing myself and answer, "But Tony, if there is an earthquake, I have to smell like a rose!" We would both end up laughing. Darn that Maiello curse!

But Tony understood me, he really understood me. I don't believe anyone truly understood me except for my precious husband Tony, my children, and a handful of other people.

Mamma was right; the war did eventually come about— World War II. Tony was conscripted and served in the Army, 13th Regiment, First Armored Division. His tour of duty started in England and Ireland, and lasted four and a half years. He went on to North Africa in the African Campaign when his regiment was attached to the British Afrika Corps. He also served in French Morocco, Algeria, Tunisia and then went on to Anzio, Italy.

Tony served under General Clark in the Italian campaign. The Palazzo Reale in Caserta was General Clark's headquarters, and Caserta served as the Mediterranean headquarters of all the allied forces. Tony was in the battles in Naples, Foggia, the North Apennines, the Po Valley, Rome, and the Arno.

When Tony was stationed in the Caserta area he visited both his hometown of San Benedetto and mine. He even met my two grandmothers and all my aunts, uncles and cousins! He showed them all a picture of me, all grown up, that he carried with him throughout the war, and told them that he loved me and was going home to marry me.

Tony was at the battle of Monte Cassino and finished the war in Lake Como, Northern Italy, bringing home with him a picture of the dead Mussolini and his dead mistress, Clara Petacci, among his many souvenirs.

The eventual surrender of the German army was signed in the Palazzo Reale on April 29, 1945. And to think we had our Easter picnics there!

But now I've gotten ahead of my story.

Mamma and Papa went on to produce three more children in America. Mamma lived to the age of eighty-two, long enough to watch us all mature, marry and give her sixteen grandchildren and seven great grandchildren. She eventually told them her stories too! Mamma loved these grandchildren greatly. And the Maiello genes and the "disease" of cleanliness are still with us today in these grandchildren. Many will see themselves in those stories.

Lastly, on Papa, well my father turned out to be not as we expected. But in all fairness to him I know that a tremendous adjustment was required of him with our arrival in America, just as we were trying to adjust to a new land and language.

The timing was terrible. The Great Depression of the 1930s took away within one year all of whatever treasures we had brought from Italy. Papa lost his compensation case and times got very bad. There was no work for him and no money, as with many other people during those rough years.

We soon learned that he was a very complex and tortured human being, and with great disappointment we learned also that we had to make our own way in life. What was meant to be parental authority on his part led only to anger and great resentment in us. We were strangers to each other and he was in command.

He was treating us like little children and we were just too mature to be treated that way. We weren't accustomed to being told what to do; we knew what to do. You could not reason with him. His mind was set to his way only, with no getting through to him. We were fighting a losing battle.

My expectations of a papa soon fell far short of the reality of having gotten one I couldn't forgive for not being all I expected him to be.

Mamma's once-dominant and powerful personality became submissive in America, due to the poverty that we were subjected to and the fact that Papa just didn't know us. It humbled her. We children weren't happy and she began to wonder if she had done the right thing in coming to America. We were unhappy and angry but our anger didn't diminish our love for her. We didn't realize how much we would miss the joyful richness of the life we had in Italy. We were cut off from all that we knew of a special, loving existence with all the relatives and friends there. They sent pictures of themselves along with their letters to Mamma. Sadly, as I was growing up I never realized they missed us as much as we missed them. Only now do I realize how many silent tears were shed on each side of the ocean, how painful it was for all.

Times were very difficult, and I choose to refer to the 1930s as the lost years: lost childhood, lost love, loss of innocence.

But I will say that the four of us worked; Mamma on a sewing machine in our apartment and my brothers and I at odd jobs after school. Ciccillo said he was happy to go shining shoes, he enjoyed the independence it gave him. When he made two dollars, he kept a nickel and gave Mamma the rest.

Then he and Mimi got jobs in a florist's shop on Montague Street. They worked together delivering flowers until Mimi returned to school. Underage, I worked cleaning strings off blouses in a factory. We gave Mamma the few pennies we made at our jobs so that she could buy food and pay the rent.

Our lives became a little better once we graduated school and went on to full-time jobs, still handing over our salaries to help Mamma, Papa and their growing second family. Papa was diagnosed with a heart condition. He tried to work sporadically at odd jobs but reached the point where he was just too ill.

With the passage of years, and our inevitable adulthood, we watched a change in Papa. He started to mellow, and the love and attention that we missed from him as children was bestowed upon our three younger siblings when he learned what being a papa truly meant. He learned finally to love, and to watch them grow, and participate in their upbringing, something that he had missed with us.

Then, Ciccillo fell head-over-heels in love with Antoinette and married her on April 20, 1940. She was his first, great and only love.

I met my Tony on May 8, 1941 through his very great friend John, John's girlfriend, who was my friend Katie, and my new sister-in-law, Antoinette. Tony and I saw each other for three months until he was conscripted and went to boot camp in Fort Dix, New Jersey.

Three months later, after maneuvers in the south, he was given two weeks' leave before he shipped out to England. At that time I was introduced to his large family. I was pleased with them because I saw a little bit of him in each of them. His mother, my eventual mother-in-law, was an exceptionally wonderful, loving person. We had an excellent rapport and loved each other dearly. Tony and I promised to write to each other while he was away. It became a long-distance love affair.

My brother Mimi did go through life with a clear head and also with a pure heart. He loved everyone, saw no malice in anyone and many loved him back. He was also quite the ladies' man.

On the other hand, Ciccillo and I were the silent ones, more reserved, analyzing people before forming an opinion. Most of the time we were right in our observations, but also able to turn the other cheek "seven-times-seventy." And, we were also able to love very much.

Then America entered World War II when the Japanese bombed Pearl Harbor in December 1941. Ciccillo and Mimi went into service, both feeling enough patriotism to volunteer their services in the United States Navy. And Ciccillo was by then a married man with a three-and-a-half-year-old son. Ciccillo worked in communications as a radioman in the South Pacific, seeing the island of Saipan and many of the Philippine islands on the ship U.S.S. Appalachian. The Appalachian was a flagship, with Admiral Nimitz aboard. Mimi served on the destroyer U.S.S. Nelson. His tour of duty was primarily in Europe and, toward the end of the war, in the South Pacific.

After the war they both came home safely, along with my Tony, who, despite having suffered a shrapnel wound in his head in North Africa, had continued the Italian Campaign. They patched him up and sent him back into the field. He returned in 1945, before the armistice was signed, and we married on March 9, 1946.

When Mimi returned from his service in the Navy and finally met Anita, we knew that he was hooked. He put her on a pedestal from that day on, and married her on September 6, 1947.

Papa's heart was changed further with the grandchildren we three gave him. He loved Frank Jr., Vivian, Dominick Jr. and especially my daughter Toni. He loved her most of all.

By the time my daughter Linda was born, Papa lovingly gave her a bottle of milk, something that he had never done for any of his six children.

With Papa's maturity and change of heart and the love that he showed my daughters, there was finally forgiveness in my heart for him, so much forgiveness that I eventually named my third daughter Julia in his honor.

With the sad irony of life once again Mamma was left with three children to raise when Papa died at the age of fifty-six. At his funeral I told Mimi's wife, Anita, that I asked God to absolve Papa of all his sins and give them to me.

With great compassion and understanding, Ciccillo, Mimi and I had succeeded in becoming good human beings, parents and citizens in spite of the difficult situation we had lived through, thanks to Mamma and our early years in Italy.

But, in all honesty, I truly believe that Papa loved us in his own way.

e' la comedia e' finita

ITALIAN QUOTATIONS

In 'Grammatical Italian', Neapolitan and Sicilian Dialect

I have often been asked to put some of the following quotations down on paper. I would like to share them with you.

You have to remember that in my youth we lived by these quotes. They were like our Bible. They were embedded in our young brains.

If you were deciding to do something, you didn't just jump in. You considered first is this good or bad? Your split-second decision was your free choice. That's what is given to us on the instant of conception.

"*Non sputa in cielo, che in faccia torna.*"
"Don't spit in the sky, it will fall flat in your face."
Or, "What goes around comes around."

"*I morti testa con testa e i vivi fanno festa.*"
"The dead are placed head to head and the live ones have a feast."

"*Male chi more.*"
"The live ones manage to live."

"*Una mamma campo cienti figlie, ma cienti figlie non campono una mamma.*"
"A mother can take care of one hundred children, but one hundred children cannot take care of one mother."

"I*ennero e nipoti quelle che fai e tutto perduto.*"
"What grandparents do for children, when grown up the children soon forget; all is forgotten."

"*Fa bene e scordati, fa male e penzaci.*"
"Do good and forget it, do bad and think about it."

"*Sula' a cucchiara sape che sta inda tiana.*"
"Only the spoon knows what's in the pot."

"*U cano sempre mozzica u struppiato.*"
" A dog always bites a poor man dressed in rags."
This means that both man and dog always pick on the man already down. It also means, when you're down you just can't win.

"*Si cambia la via vecchia per nuovo, sape che' lassa ma non sape che' trova.*"
"Don't change the old road for the new. You know what you have, but don't know what you will find."

"*A frivere, siante a dore.*"
"In the frying, you get the odor."
This has nothing to do with food at all. It means that you will only know a person's worth or a situation's outcome by careful examination.

"*Vizzio di natura fina a morte dure.*"
"Habits of nature stay with you until you die."
Meaning, no one really changes.

"*Il mondo finisce quanto l` uomo vole.*"
"The end of the world will come when men can fly!"

"*Vai cuna funa g`nanna.*"
"You are going at this with a noose around your neck!"
This is said to someone who is going to do something against his will.

"*Chi e nato tunno non more quadro.*"
"If you are born round, you will not die square."
Don't expect people to change; they won't.

"*Si vena a morta non ti trova.*"
"If death comes it won't find you!"
This is said to a person who is never home no matter what time of day you try to reach him.
Death will find you anywhere, of course, but it feels so good when you tell the person involved; it's so satisfying in Italian, especially if you say it between your clenched teeth!

"*A volpe perde u pilo, ma no u vizzio.*"
"A fox changes his fur but not his habits; be alert at all times."

"*Chi va piano va sano e va lontano.*"
"He who goes slow, goes safe and far."

"*Meglio sulo che male accumpagniata.*"
"Better to be alone than in bad company."

THE FAMILIES

David Veccia
Carmela Veccia
siblings of:
SEBASTIANO VECCIA —— m. RAFFAELA PETRUCCI

Maria Antonia Petrucci
sibling of:
m. RAFFAELA PETRUCCI

their children:
Rocco Veccia m. Michela
daughter: Filomena

*VINCENZA VECCIA

Filomena Veccia m. Pasquale Izzo

Carolina Veccia m. Antonio Venerio

Nicola Veccia m. Nannina
daughter: Rafaellina

*VINCENZA VECCIA m. GIULIO MAIELLO
Italian born children: **Francesco** (Ciccillo), **Domenico** (Mimi) & **Maria Marzia**
American-born children: **Anna, Vito & Gene**

Angela Maria Maiello
(Brazilian)
cousin of:
FRANCESCO MAIELLO m.
MARZIA SPARACO

their children:
Domenico Maiello m. Serafina
daughters:
Marcia, Stella, Vera & Regina

Angela Maria Maiello m.
Michele Ianniello
daughter: Pupetta

Filippo Maiello m.
Esperanza
daughter: Marzia

*GIULIO MAIELLO
Addolorada Maiello

Anna Maiello m. Antonio
Madonna
children: Sophia & Pierino
Pietro Maiello

Margarita Maiello m.
Antonio Madonna
Eduardo Maiello

Carmela Maiello m. Paolo
Ganzerli
Francesco Maiello

AUTHOR'S NOTES

A Special 'Thank-you'

My dear Mom, Maria Marzia, for your tremendous love, sharp memory and great attention to detail. I'm thankful that your desire to share your early years in Italy with all your nieces and nephews coincided with my desire to share them with everyone. By giving them a peek into your life with Mamma before you came to America, I watched you relive your youth. It was charming and endearing.

When I asked you to "Think as a child and speak as a child," sometimes pushing you too far, you always rebounded with angelic perseverance. And you finally learned how to cry! I salute you and celebrate your life with great appreciation for your strength, and will always love you. I respectfully extend for you your heartfelt thanks to all the friends who traveled with you on this journey through life.

My dear Dad, for your eternal love, and for always showing me the richness of life by being "A Count of most fortunate account" in the wealth of people that loved you. I salute you, respect you and will always love you.

My dear Charles, I am thankful for our special love and greatly appreciate your unending support in keeping me focused, for being my ballast during this emotional roller-coaster ride, and for your work on the Maiello house sketch.

My dear Linda, for your love, your offer of editorial services, and your peaches-and-cream complexion with three shades of green eyes.

My dear Julie, my curly titian-haired baby who grew up so quickly, for your love and tolerance, your steadfast spirit, and your artwork and suggestions for the cover.

Bob and John, for loving my sisters.

Uncle Frankie (Ciccillo), for always being a perfect, loving uncle and a wonderful, caring brother to my mother. Aunt Antoinette, for your love and great enthusiasm about this work.

Uncle Dominick (Mimi), for his great passion for life and great kindness to my sister Julie. Aunt Anita, for your love and for sharing your pictures and sweet memories.

Aunt Anna, for always being Nanny to me, and Uncle Adolph, for your love and for always being there for my parents and me.

Uncle Vito, for your loving ways of creating laughter and mirth, and always bringing bread. Aunt Eileen, for our twenty-two years working together and our own laughter and tears.

Uncle Gene, despite the fact that you murdered all my dolls when I was a little girl, you were always the greatly loved older brother we lacked, who graciously shared Grandpa's passport, your personal research on Maiello Heraldry and other memorabilia with me. I still don't forgive you for killing my dolls. Aunt Stella, for the way your face lights up with laughter and for noticing the color of my mother's slippers and always commenting on it.

All the Ciccillo, Mimi and Maria descendants, my special cousins and sisters, who share with me the immigrant connection, and our spouses and children for showing great interest in and support for this work, and great patience for the time it took to complete it. To Frank, Liz, Vivian, Steve, Don, Kathy, Chuck, Linda, Bob, Michele, Pete, Julie, John, Marie, Danny, Geanine, Nicole, Anthony, Anjanette, Frank, Karen, Jaime, David, Jon, Andrew and little Mary Faith.

Especially you, Vivian, with your great exuberance and love! And for giving our family its first doctor, your daughter, Nicole.

The rest of my wonderful cousins, the children born to the American-born, their spouses and children, that you may appreciate our rich heritage with this gift from my mother. To John, Claudia, Vic, Michelle, Tony, Linda, Michael, Karen, Roxane, Michael, Ritchie, Joe, Ann Marie, Vincent, Wendy, Matthew, Christina, Nicholas, Sabrina, Brianna, Grant, Christopher and little Tyler Michael.

Our Brazilian cousins, with the knowledge that through the generations and distance we have kept our family closeness.

Mom's first cousins, Domenico and Serafina's daughter's and their spouses, Marcia and Helber, Stella and Jorge, Vera and Puppe, and Regina and Aldo. Through Stella's husband Jorge Correa, the airline pilot, we developed and maintained contact with our second cousins, their daughters, Ana Maria and Claudia, and Ana Maria's children, Daniela and Marcelo.

To another very special cousin who came into our lives when Ana Maria married Armido Mastrogiovanni, a most charming and loving doctor, who gave us yet another cousin, Bruna, who's as pretty as the Mona Lisa!

Thank you, Armido, for regaling us with stories about your wife's grandparents, Domenico and Serafina. To hear of the respect, pride and love for Domenico Maiello in Brazil was greatly appreciated.

And for being doubly blessed with thirty first cousins on the Sparano side of the family. Along with special aunts and uncles who shared fun parties, picnics, country houses in Candlewood Lake and Shannarock, Brooklyn, Huntington, Patchogue, lunch in Manhattan and very much laughter. My only regret is that I wish I could have shared this with Aunt Edith.

My godparents, John and Katherine Mone, and their daughters, for all the laughter we shared together.

My in-laws, Phyllis and Joe Seiler, and my lovely nieces, Tracy and Jennifer.

Terry and Lucille Guecia and The TL Club memories. Joane Olsen Quan, who returns to Long Island each summer so we can laugh together again. Karen Horton Striano, who insists I'm the only friend left in New York that she loves!

Jean Soldo, daughter of "the lady in black," for your knowledge of the Italian language, your help with the quotations, and for your sons, Bob and Ron, my childhood friends. Along with the two Tonys and Grandmas our families certainly spent many happy days together! I'm glad for the timely manner in which Bob and I spoke of this work. Requiescat in pace.

Fay Romano, for your love, constant support and our years of working together.

Randee Schwartz-Locke, for your friendship, love and gracious support. Here's to yet another adventure to celebrate together!

Linda Flannery, for your friendship, kindness and your research on Vanvitelli.

To my editor, John Fremont, a transplanted Brooklynite, I appreciate your suggestions and most charming correspondence; and to Joe Shaw, for a sensitive, wonderful editing job!

And last, but certainly not least, Kim McCormick.

BIBLIOGRAPHY

Norberg-Schulz, Christian. *Late Baroque and Rococo Architecture.* (1974).

Garzanti Comprehensive Dictionary, Italian-English. Italy. McGraw-Hill Book Co., Inc., (1961).

Wittkower, Rudolf. *Art and Architecture in Italy, 1600-1750,* 3rd ed., (1973).

"The History of Italy." *The World Book Encyclopedia.* USA. Field Enterprises, Inc., (1954).

"History of the Bourbon Family." "Italian History." "King Humberto." "King Victor Emmanuel III." "Mussolini." "Mt. Vesuvius." Microsoft Encarta. Funk & Wagnalls Corporation, (1994).

"Luigi Vanvitelli." *Grolier's Encyclopedia.* Grolier Electronic Publishing, Inc., (1995).

Epilogue: "e' la comedia e' finita," *I Pugliacci,* Ruggiero Leoncavallo